365 Hebrew Words

The Language of the Old Testament Bible

365 Hebrew Words

The Language of the Old Testament Bible

Vinu V Das

Tip

Tabor Press

978-0-9940194-7-9

- **Meaning:** Ground, Earth

- **Bible Reference:** Genesis 2:7 – *"Then the Lord God formed a man from the dust of the ground."*

Message: The Hebrew word **Adamah** means "ground" or "earth," from which God formed Adam. This word reminds us of our humble origins—we are dust, yet God breathed life into us. While we are made from the earth, we are also created in His image, given purpose and responsibility. **Adamah** also reminds us of our dependence on God; without Him, we return to dust. Yet, through Christ, we are given eternal life. Stay humble, knowing your true worth is found in God.

Reflection Questions for the Day:

1. What does it mean to be made from the dust?

2. How can you balance humility with your identity in God?

3. How does knowing your origin affect how you treat others?

Day 7: Shabbat (שַׁבָּת)

- **Meaning:** Sabbath, Rest

- **Bible Reference:** Genesis 2:2 – *"On the seventh day God rested from all His work."*

Message: God set apart the **Shabbat** (Sabbath) as a day of rest. He did not rest because He was tired but to establish a pattern for us. In a world that glorifies busyness, Sabbath reminds us to trust in God's provision. Jesus declared that He is the Lord of the Sabbath (Mark 2:28), offering true rest for our souls. Taking time to pause and worship refocuses our

15

hearts on what truly matters. Rest is not laziness—it is obedience.

Reflection Questions for the Day:

1. Do you regularly take time to rest in God?

2. How can you incorporate Sabbath principles into your life?

3. What does true rest in Christ mean to you?

Week 1 Conclusion

From the beginning of time, God has revealed Himself as the sovereign Creator, bringing order, purpose, and life into existence. His power and presence are evident in the heavens, the earth, and in humanity itself. The Spirit of God moves actively, breathing life into what was once empty and shaping all things with divine intention. His light overcomes darkness, illuminating truth and guiding us into His ways. As beings formed from the earth yet created in His image, we are called to reflect His creativity, wisdom, and love. The concept of rest reminds us that our trust should not be in our own efforts but in His sustaining grace. By embracing the truths revealed in creation, we gain a deeper understanding of who He is and how we are meant to live in relationship with Him.

Week 2: The Nature and Character of God

Day 8: Adonai (אֲדֹנָי)

- **Meaning:** Lord, Master

- **Bible Reference:** Psalm 8:1 – *"O Lord (Adonai), our Lord, how majestic is Your name in all the earth!"*

Message: The Hebrew word **Adonai** means "Lord" or "Master," signifying authority, rulership, and ownership. In ancient times, a master had full authority over his servants, and they depended on him for provision and protection. When we call God **Adonai**, we acknowledge Him as the rightful ruler of our lives. Too often, we want God as our Savior but struggle to submit to Him as Lord. Yet, surrendering to **Adonai** brings freedom—His leadership is perfect, and His care is unwavering. The more we trust Him as our Master, the more we experience His provision and peace. Are you truly allowing **Adonai** to lead your life?

Reflection Questions for the Day:

1. In what ways do you struggle to let God be Lord over your life?

2. How does recognizing God as **Adonai** bring security and peace?

3. What would it look like to fully submit to God's authority?

Day 9: Chesed (חֶסֶד)

- **Meaning:** Lovingkindness, Mercy, Covenant Love

- **Bible Reference:** Lamentations 3:22 – *"The steadfast love (chesed) of the Lord never ceases; His mercies never come to an end."*

Message: Chesed is one of the most powerful words in the Hebrew Bible. It describes God's steadfast, loyal, and merciful love toward His people. Unlike human love, which often depends on emotions or circumstances, **chesed** is unwavering and covenantal. Even when Israel was unfaithful, God remained faithful because of His **chesed**. This love is fully revealed in Jesus, who demonstrated ultimate **chesed** by dying for our sins. When we experience God's **chesed**, it changes us—we are called to show the same faithful love to others. Today, reflect on how deeply God loves you, and let that love flow through you to others.

Reflection Questions for the Day:

1. How have you experienced God's **chesed** in your life?

2. What makes God's love different from human love?

3. How can you show **chesed** to others, even when they don't deserve it?

Day 10: Emunah (אֱמוּנָה)

- **Meaning:** Faith, Faithfulness

- **Bible Reference:** Habakkuk 2:4 – *"The righteous shall live by his faith (emunah)."*

Message: Emunah is not just belief—it is **faithfulness** in action. In Hebrew thought, faith is not merely intellectual agreement but a steadfast commitment to trust and obey God. Abraham showed **emunah** when he followed God into the unknown. The Israelites were called to walk in **emunah**, even when circumstances seemed impossible. Jesus calls us to the same kind of faith—one that trusts beyond sight and remains faithful in trials. When life is uncertain, hold fast to **emunah**, knowing that God is faithful even when we struggle.

Reflection Questions for the Day:

1. How would you describe your faith—intellectual belief or active trust?

2. In what area do you need to grow in **emunah**?

3. How does God's faithfulness strengthen your own faith?

Day 11: Kadosh (קָדוֹשׁ)

- **Meaning:** Holy, Set Apart

- **Bible Reference:** Isaiah 6:3 – *"Holy, holy, holy (kadosh) is the Lord of hosts; the whole earth is full of His glory!"*

Message: Kadosh means "holy" or "set apart." God is completely pure, perfect, and beyond all comparison. When Isaiah saw a vision of God's holiness, he was overwhelmed, realizing his own sinfulness. Yet, God's holiness is not just something to admire—it is something we are called to reflect. As His people, we are to live **kadosh**, different from the world, displaying His character. Holiness is not just about avoiding sin; it is about being fully devoted to God. Are you living a life that reflects God's holiness?

Reflection Questions for the Day:

1. What does it mean for you to be "set apart" for God?

2. How can you grow in holiness without falling into legalism?

3. What is one area of your life that needs to be surrendered to God's holiness?

Day 12: Shalom (שָׁלוֹם)

- **Meaning:** Peace, Wholeness, Completeness

- **Bible Reference:** Numbers 6:26 – *"The Lord lift up His countenance upon you and give you peace (shalom)."*

Message: Shalom is more than just the absence of conflict—it means **wholeness, completeness, and well-being**. In a broken world, true **shalom** can only come from God. Jesus, the Prince of Peace, brings the ultimate **shalom** by reconciling us to the Father. When we walk in **shalom**, we experience inner peace despite outward chaos. This peace is not passive; it actively restores, heals, and brings harmony. If you are feeling anxious today, turn to the One who gives perfect **shalom**.

Reflection Questions for the Day:

1. What is stealing your peace right now?

2. How does Jesus bring true **shalom** into your life?

3. How can you be an agent of **shalom** in the world?

Day 13: Tzedakah (צְ דָ קָ ה)

- **Meaning:** Righteousness, Justice, Charity

- **Bible Reference:** Proverbs 21:3 – *"To do righteousness (tzedakah) and justice is more acceptable to the Lord than sacrifice."*

Message: Tzedakah means righteousness, but it also carries the idea of justice and generosity. In Hebrew culture, righteousness was not just about personal morality—it involved caring for the poor and acting justly. God calls His people to be **tzedakah**, reflecting His justice and compassion in a world filled with oppression. Jesus embodied **tzedakah**, caring for the marginalized and challenging corrupt systems. As His followers, we are to live justly, love mercy, and walk humbly before God.

Reflection Questions for the Day:

1. How does biblical righteousness differ from the world's idea of morality?

2. What practical ways can you practice **tzedakah** in your community?

3. Are there any areas where you need to align more with God's justice?

Day 14: Yeshua (יֵשׁוּעַ)

- **Meaning:** Salvation, Deliverance

- **Bible Reference:** Isaiah 12:2 – *"The Lord is my strength and my song; He has become my salvation (yeshua)."*

Message: The name **Yeshua** means "salvation" and is the Hebrew name of Jesus. In the Old Testament, **yeshua** often refers to God's deliverance, both physically and spiritually. Jesus is the ultimate fulfillment of **yeshua**, rescuing humanity from sin and death. Through His sacrifice, we are given eternal salvation, not by works but by grace. If you have received **Yeshua**, you have been set free. If not, today is the day to call on Him and be saved!

Reflection Questions for the Day:

1. What does salvation mean to you personally?

2. Have you fully embraced the freedom that comes with **Yeshua**?

3. How can you share the message of **yeshua** with others?

Week 2 Conclusion

The second week of study has deepened our understanding of God's nature and His relationship with us. We have explored His role as our sovereign ruler, His unwavering love, and the faithfulness that sustains us in all circumstances. His holiness calls us to live differently, reflecting His purity and purpose in our daily lives. The peace He offers is not just the absence of turmoil but a deep wholeness that comes from being in harmony with Him. His justice is not only about fairness but about living with generosity and compassion toward others. Most importantly, we have seen how His saving power is fully revealed in the One who rescues and redeems. As we continue to grow in knowledge and faith, may we not only acknowledge these truths but also apply them in the way we live, love, and serve.

Week 3: Walking in God's Ways

Day 15: Torah (תּוֹרָ ה)

- **Meaning:** Law, Instruction, Teaching

- **Bible Reference:** Joshua 1:8 – *"This Book of the Law (Torah) shall not depart from your mouth, but you shall meditate on it day and night."*

Message: Torah means more than just "law"—it refers to God's instruction and teaching. It is His divine guidance for how His people should live. While the Torah includes the laws given to Israel, it also reflects God's heart and wisdom. Jesus did not come to abolish the Torah but to fulfill it (Matthew 5:17). When we meditate on God's Word, we are transformed, aligning our lives with His will. The **Torah** is not about legalism but about love—God lovingly shows us the best way to live. Do you delight in God's teachings as your guide?

Reflection Questions for the Day:

1. How do you view God's laws—burdensome rules or loving guidance?

2. What steps can you take to meditate on God's Word daily?

3. How does following God's instruction bring life and freedom?

Day 16: Dabar (דָּ בָ ר)

- **Meaning:** Word, Matter, Thing

- **Bible Reference:** Deuteronomy 8:3 – *"Man shall not live by bread alone, but by every word (dabar) that proceeds from the mouth of the Lord."*

Message: Dabar means "word," but it also signifies action and reality. In Scripture, God's **dabar** is not just speech—it is power. When God speaks, things happen. Creation itself was formed by His **dabar** (Genesis 1). Jesus, the Word (John 1:1), embodies this truth—what He speaks brings life. If God's **dabar** is so powerful, how much more should we trust in His promises? Let His Word shape your thoughts, decisions, and direction.

Reflection Questions for the Day:

1. How do you respond to God's **dabar** in your life?

2. Are there any areas where you struggle to trust God's promises?

3. How can you speak words of life and faith today?

Day 17: Shema (שְׁ מַ עַ)

- **Meaning:** Hear, Listen, Obey

- **Bible Reference:** Deuteronomy 6:4 – *"Hear (Shema), O Israel: The Lord our God, the Lord is one."*

Message: Shema means more than just "hear"—it means to listen with the intent to obey. The famous **Shema** prayer in Deuteronomy 6:4-5 calls Israel to love and obey God completely. In Hebrew thought, true listening leads to action. Jesus echoed this when He said, *"He who has ears to hear, let him hear!"* (Matthew 11:15). Many hear God's Word, but few truly listen. Today, ask yourself: Am I merely hearing, or am I obeying?

Reflection Questions for the Day:

1. What is one area where God is calling you to obey?

2. Do you approach Scripture just to hear it, or to live it out?

3. How can you develop a heart that truly listens to God?

Day 18: Halak (ה‎ָל‎ַך‎)

- **Meaning:** Walk, Live, Conduct Oneself

- **Bible Reference:** Micah 6:8 – *"Walk (halak) humbly with your God."*

Message: In Hebrew, **halak** means "to walk" but also refers to a way of life. To "walk with God" is to live in daily relationship with Him. Micah 6:8 calls us to **halak** humbly, acting with justice and mercy. Faith is not just about belief— it's about a journey. Jesus called His disciples to follow Him, not just to listen. Is your **halak** aligned with God's path, or are you walking your own way?

Reflection Questions for the Day:

1. What does it mean for you to walk with God daily?

2. Are there areas where you are straying from God's path?

3. How can you develop a stronger walk with the Lord?

Day 19: Lev (ל‎ֵב‎)

- **Meaning:** Heart, Inner Being

- **Bible Reference:** Proverbs 4:23 – *"Above all else, guard your heart (lev), for everything you do flows from it."*

Message: The **lev** in Hebrew is more than the physical heart—it represents the mind, emotions, and will. In the

27

Bible, the **lev** is the center of decision-making. God looks at the **lev** (1 Samuel 16:7), not just outward actions. If our **lev** is right with Him, our lives will follow. Jesus taught that sin begins in the heart (Matthew 5:28), showing the importance of guarding it. What fills your **lev**? Is it aligned with God's truth?

Reflection Questions for the Day:

1. What fills your heart most—God's truth or worldly distractions?

2. How can you guard your **lev** against temptation?

3. What changes can you make to align your heart with God's?

Day 20: Yirah (יִ ר אָה)

- **Meaning:** Fear, Reverence, Awe

- **Bible Reference:** Proverbs 9:10 – *"The fear (yirah) of the Lord is the beginning of wisdom."*

Message: Yirah can mean fear, but it often refers to **reverence and awe** of God. It is not a terror that drives us away, but a holy respect that draws us closer. True wisdom begins with **yirah**—acknowledging God's greatness and our dependence on Him. Many today have lost a sense of awe toward God. When we truly grasp His majesty, our faith deepens, and obedience becomes a joy, not a burden. Let **yirah** lead you to worship today.

Reflection Questions for the Day:

1. Do you have a proper reverence for God?

2. How does the **yirah** of the Lord impact your decisions?

3. What can you do to cultivate deeper awe for God?

Day 21: Nephesh (נֶ֫פֶשׁ)

- **Meaning:** Soul, Life, Being

- **Bible Reference:** Genesis 2:7 – *"And man became a living soul (nephesh)."*

Message: Nephesh refers to the soul, the very essence of life. It is more than just a spiritual part of us—it is our whole being. When God breathed life into Adam, he became a **nephesh chayah**—a living soul. Our **nephesh** longs for God (Psalm 42:1), for only He can satisfy it. Jesus calls us to love God with all our **nephesh** (Mark 12:30). Are you living in a way that nourishes your **nephesh** in Him?

Reflection Questions for the Day:

1. What truly satisfies your soul?

2. Are you caring for your **nephesh**—spiritually, emotionally, and physically?

3. How can you love God with all your **nephesh**?

Week 3 Conclusion

Walking in God's ways is more than just following rules; it is about aligning our entire being with His truth and direction. His teachings are a guide that leads us to life, providing wisdom, clarity, and purpose. True obedience is not passive listening but an active response, demonstrating faith through action. Our relationship with God is a journey, requiring daily commitment, humility, and trust. The condition of our inner being determines the path we take, emphasizing the need to guard our thoughts, desires, and decisions. Reverence for God is the foundation of wisdom, shaping how we approach life's challenges and opportunities. As we seek Him with our whole being, we experience the fullness of His presence, guidance, and peace, ensuring that every step we take reflects His love and truth.

Week 4: God's Promises and Our Response

Day 22: Berit (בְּרִית)

- **Meaning:** Covenant, Promise, Agreement

- **Bible Reference:** Genesis 9:16 – *"The rainbow shall be in the cloud, and I will look on it to remember the everlasting covenant (berit) between God and every living creature."*

Message: A **berit** is a binding agreement, often between God and His people. The Bible is full of **berit**—God's covenant with Noah, Abraham, Moses, and ultimately, the New Covenant through Jesus. Unlike human contracts, God's **berit** is based on His faithfulness, not our performance. The ultimate **berit** is salvation through Christ, sealed with His blood (Luke 22:20). When we trust in His **berit**, we find security in His unchanging promises. Are you living in the assurance of God's covenant today?

Reflection Questions for the Day:

1. What does it mean to live under God's covenant?

2. How does the **berit** through Jesus change your relationship with God?

3. Are there any areas where you need to trust in God's promises more?

Day 23: Ahavah (אַהֲבָה)

- **Meaning:** Love, Deep Affection

- **Bible Reference:** Deuteronomy 6:5 – *"You shall love (ahavah) the Lord your God with all your heart, soul, and might."*

Message: Ahavah is more than a feeling—it is a commitment to act in love. God's love is not just an emotion but a covenantal love that is faithful, sacrificial, and enduring. He calls us to love Him and others with the same **ahavah** (Leviticus 19:18). Jesus embodied perfect **ahavah**, loving us to the point of giving His life. True **ahavah** seeks the good of others, even when it is difficult. Are you loving as God loves?

Reflection Questions for the Day:

1. How is **ahavah** different from the world's idea of love?

2. What are ways you can actively show love to others?

3. How can you grow in your love for God?

Day 24: Chazak (חָ_זָ_ק)

- **Meaning:** Strength, Courage, Endurance

- **Bible Reference:** Joshua 1:9 – *"Be strong (chazak) and courageous; do not be afraid, for the Lord your God is with you."*

Message: Chazak means to be strong, not just physically, but in faith and perseverance. God told Joshua to be **chazak** because He was with him. Our strength is not found in ourselves but in God's presence and promises. Life's challenges require spiritual endurance—Paul echoes this when he says, *"Be strong in the Lord" (Ephesians 6:10)*. When we trust God, we find the strength to stand firm. Are you relying on your strength or God's?

Reflection Questions for the Day:

1. What situations require **chazak** in your life right now?

33

2. How can you strengthen your faith in God?

3. What fears do you need to surrender to God's power?

Day 25: Tikvah (תִּקְוָה)

- **Meaning:** Hope, Expectation

- **Bible Reference:** Jeremiah 29:11 – *"For I know the plans I have for you... plans to give you hope (tikvah) and a future."*

Message: Tikvah means hope, not just wishful thinking but confident expectation in God's promises. In Scripture, hope is an anchor for the soul (Hebrews 6:19). Israel's hope was in God's redemption, and our hope is in Christ's return. No matter how dark the circumstances, **tikvah** in God never fails. Hope strengthens faith and renews joy. Are you placing your hope in the temporary or the eternal?

Reflection Questions for the Day:

1. What is the foundation of your **tikvah**?

2. How has God been faithful to His promises in your life?

3. How can you share hope with others?

Day 26: Rachamim (רַחֲמִים)

- **Meaning:** Mercy, Compassion, Tender Love

- **Bible Reference:** Psalm 103:8 – *"The Lord is merciful (rachamim) and gracious, slow to anger and abounding in love."*

Message: Rachamim comes from the root word for "womb," showing God's deep, motherly compassion for His people.

He does not treat us as our sins deserve but offers grace. Jesus displayed perfect **rachamim** when He healed the sick, forgave sinners, and loved the broken. We are called to show this same mercy to others (Luke 6:36). If God is merciful toward you, are you merciful toward others?

Reflection Questions for the Day:

1. How have you experienced God's **rachamim**?

2. Are there people you need to show more mercy to?

3. What does it mean to live as a reflection of God's compassion?

Day 27: Nes (נ ס)

- **Meaning:** Miracle, Sign, Banner

- **Bible Reference:** Exodus 17:15 – *"Moses built an altar and called it 'The Lord is my Banner' (Yahweh-Nissi)."*

Message: A **nes** is a visible sign of God's power, like the miracles in Egypt, the parting of the Red Sea, or the provision of manna. Miracles remind us that God is active and sovereign. Jesus performed many **nesim** (miracles) to reveal His divinity. But the greatest **nes** is salvation itself. God still works wonders today—sometimes in ways we don't expect. Are your eyes open to His miraculous work in your life?

Reflection Questions for the Day:

1. How has God shown His power in your life?

2. Do you trust God even when miracles aren't immediate?

3. How can you be a testimony of God's wonders to others?

Day 28: Shachar (שַׁ_חַ_ר)

- **Meaning:** Dawn, Morning Light

- **Bible Reference:** Psalm 30:5 – *"Weeping may last for the night, but joy comes in the morning (shachar)."*

Message: Shachar represents new beginnings. Just as morning light breaks the darkness, God brings new mercies each day (Lamentations 3:22-23). No matter how difficult the night, **shachar** promises renewal and joy. Jesus is the **Morning Star** (Revelation 22:16), bringing eternal hope. When you feel discouraged, remember that the **shachar** always comes. Trust in God's timing—His light will break through.

Reflection Questions for the Day:

1. What does the promise of **shachar** mean in your life?

2. How can you hold on to hope in difficult times?

3. What "new beginning" is God calling you to embrace?

Week 4 Conclusion

God's faithfulness is evident through His enduring covenants, showing us that His word never fails. His love is more than emotion—it is a call to commitment, drawing us into a relationship that transforms our hearts and actions. In times of uncertainty, He strengthens us, encouraging us to stand firm in courage rather than fear. True hope is not rooted in circumstances but in His unshakable promises, providing security even in the darkest seasons. His mercy reminds us that we are forgiven, and as recipients of His grace, we are called to extend the same compassion to others. God's wonders, whether miraculous or subtle, reveal His presence, reminding us that He is actively working in our lives. Just as the morning light brings renewal, His timing is perfect, ensuring that no matter how long the night, joy will always come in Him.

Week 5: Worship and Drawing Near to God

Day 29: Avodah (עֲבוֹדָה)

- **Meaning:** Work, Service, Worship

- **Bible Reference:** Exodus 3:12 – *"When you have brought the people out of Egypt, you will worship (avodah) God on this mountain."*

Message: In Hebrew, **avodah** means both "work" and "worship," showing that true worship is not just singing but serving God with our whole lives. The Israelites were freed from slavery so they could **avodah**—serve and worship God. Jesus taught that worship is in spirit and truth (John 4:24), not just rituals. Every act of obedience, every job done for God's glory, is **avodah**. If our work and worship are separate, we are missing true devotion. Is your daily life an act of worship?

Reflection Questions for the Day:

1. How can you turn your daily work into worship?

2. What does it mean to serve God in all aspects of life?

3. Do you see worship as only singing, or as a lifestyle?

Day 30: Mizbeach (מִזְבֵּחַ)

- **Meaning:** Altar, Place of Sacrifice

- **Bible Reference:** Genesis 8:20 – *"Then Noah built an altar (mizbeach) to the Lord."*

Message: A **mizbeach** is an altar, where sacrifices were offered to God as acts of worship and devotion. In the Old Testament, altars were built as memorials to God's faithfulness. In the New Testament, we are called to be "living sacrifices" (Romans 12:1), offering our lives as an act of worship. Worship requires surrender—what are you placing on the **mizbeach**? True worship is costly, but it draws us closer to God. What do you need to surrender today?

Reflection Questions for the Day:

1. What does it mean to be a "living sacrifice"?

2. Is there anything in your life you need to place on the **mizbeach**?

3. How can sacrifice be an act of worship?

Day 31: Tehillah (תְּהִלָּה)

- **Meaning:** Praise, Song of Worship

- **Bible Reference:** Psalm 22:3 – *"You are enthroned on the praises (tehillah) of Israel."*

Message: Tehillah refers to praise, often in the form of spontaneous singing. The Psalms are full of **tehillah**, showing that worship is an overflow of the heart. God is "enthroned" in our praise, meaning He dwells where He is worshiped. Worship shifts our focus from problems to God's greatness. **Tehillah** is not just about singing—it's about declaring who God is. Are you making praise a daily habit?

Reflection Questions for the Day:

1. How does worship change your perspective in difficult times?

2. What are ways you can praise God outside of church?

3. How can you cultivate a heart of **tehillah**?

Day 32: Qadosh (קָדוֹשׁ)

- **Meaning:** Set Apart, Holy

- **Bible Reference:** Leviticus 19:2 – *"Be holy (qadosh), for I the Lord your God am holy."*

Message: Qadosh means to be set apart for God. Worship is not just singing—it's living in a way that honors God's holiness. Many want to worship God but still live like the world. True worship leads to transformation, making us more like Him. Holiness is not perfection; it is devotion to God. Does your life reflect a heart that is truly set apart?

Reflection Questions for the Day:

1. How does holiness relate to worship?

2. Are there areas in your life that need to be set apart for God?

3. What does it mean to live a life of worship?

Day 33: Zamar (זָמַר)

- **Meaning:** To Sing, Play Music in Praise

- **Bible Reference:** Psalm 98:5 – *"Sing praises (zamar) to the Lord with the lyre, with the lyre and the sound of melody."*

Message: Zamar means to worship through music. The Bible is full of instruments being used in praise—David played the harp, trumpets were blown in worship, and songs were written to glorify God. Worship through music stirs the soul and draws us closer to God. But true **zamar** is not just about melody—it's about the heart behind the music. Do you worship God with joy and sincerity?

Reflection Questions for the Day:

1. How does music help you connect with God?

2. What role does praise play in your relationship with Him?

3. How can you incorporate **zamar** into your daily worship?

Day 34: Yadah (יָדָ֫ה)

- **Meaning:** To Give Thanks, To Worship with Raised Hands

- **Bible Reference:** Psalm 100:4 – *"Enter His gates with thanksgiving (yadah) and His courts with praise."*

Message: Yadah is an expression of thanksgiving and surrender. In Hebrew culture, lifting hands was a sign of trust, surrender, and celebration. Worship is not just about singing—it's about posture. Lifting hands in **yadah** signifies yielding to God's authority and thanking Him in all circumstances. Do you approach God with a heart full of gratitude?

Reflection Questions for the Day:

1. How does gratitude impact your worship?

2. Are you holding back in surrendering to God?

3. What can you thank God for today?

Day 35: Ruach HaKodesh (רוּחַ הַקֹּ֫דֶשׁ)

- **Meaning:** The Holy Spirit, The Spirit of Holiness

- **Bible Reference:** Isaiah 63:10 – *"They rebelled and grieved His Holy Spirit (Ruach HaKodesh)."*

Message: Ruach HaKodesh is the Holy Spirit, the very presence of God moving in worship. In the Old Testament, He empowered prophets and leaders. In the New Testament, He fills believers, guiding and empowering them to worship in spirit and truth. Worship is not just an action—it is communion with **Ruach HaKodesh**. Are you allowing Him to move in your worship?

Reflection Questions for the Day:

1. How does the Holy Spirit influence your worship?

2. Do you seek the presence of **Ruach HaKodesh** daily?

3. How can you allow the Spirit to lead you in worship?

Week 5 Conclusion

This week's words reveal that worship is more than just music—it is a way of life. **Avodah** shows that work can be worship, and **mizbeach** reminds us that worship requires sacrifice. Through **tehillah** and **zamar**, we express praise, but worship also involves **qadosh**—living set apart for God. **Yadah** teaches us that thanksgiving is central to true worship, and the presence of **Ruach HaKodesh** makes our worship alive and powerful. Worship is not about performance—it's about communion with God. May we live lives of worship that honor and glorify Him in everything we do!

Week 6: The Power of God's Presence

Day 36: Shekinah (שׁ.כ.ינ.ה)

- **Meaning:** Dwelling, Divine Presence

- **Bible Reference:** Exodus 40:34 – *"Then the cloud covered the Tent of Meeting, and the glory of the Lord filled the tabernacle."*

Message: Shekinah refers to God's visible, manifest presence among His people. In the Old Testament, His presence was seen in the cloud and fire that led Israel. His presence was in the Tabernacle, and later, in the Temple. Jesus revealed the fullness of God's presence, and now, through the Holy Spirit, believers are the dwelling place of God. His presence is not confined to buildings—it is with us. When we seek Him, we experience His **Shekinah** in our lives.

Reflection Questions for the Day:

1. How aware are you of God's presence in your daily life?

2. What areas of your life need to be more centered on His presence?

3. How can you cultivate a deeper awareness of God's **Shekinah**?

Day 37: Kavod (כ.בוד)

- **Meaning:** Glory, Honor, Weight of God's Presence

- **Bible Reference:** Psalm 24:8 – *"Who is this King of glory (kavod)? The Lord strong and mighty, the Lord mighty in battle."*

Message: Kavod describes the weighty, majestic presence of God. It is His honor, splendor, and power revealed. When the priests ministered in the Temple, God's **kavod** filled the room so powerfully that they could not stand. The same **kavod** that covered Mount Sinai is now revealed through Jesus. His glory is not distant—it transforms us. Do you long to experience the **kavod** of God?

Reflection Questions for the Day:

1. How have you experienced God's **kavod** in your life?

2. What does it mean for your life to reflect His glory?

3. How can you live in a way that honors His **kavod**?

Day 38: Panim (פָּ נִ ים)

- **Meaning:** Face, Presence

- **Bible Reference:** Exodus 33:14 – *"My presence (panim) will go with you, and I will give you rest."*

Message: Panim literally means "face," but it also symbolizes the presence of God. Moses longed for God's **panim** and refused to move without it. Seeing God's face represents intimacy with Him. In Jesus, we see the fullness of God's **panim**, and through the Holy Spirit, we experience His presence daily. Are you seeking His face or just His blessings?

Reflection Questions for the Day:

1. What does seeking God's **panim** mean in your daily life?

2. How can you deepen your relationship with Him?

3. Do you desire His presence more than what He can give?

Day 39: Makom (מָקוֹם)

- **Meaning:** Place, Sacred Space

- **Bible Reference:** Genesis 28:16 – *"Surely the Lord is in this place (makom), and I did not know it."*

Message: Makom refers to a place, but it also represents the space where God meets us. Jacob encountered God in a **makom** and realized that God had been there all along. Worship is not confined to a temple or church—God meets us in the everyday moments of life. Any space can become sacred when we recognize His presence. Are you aware of God in the places you inhabit?

Reflection Questions for the Day:

1. Have you ever had a personal encounter with God in an unexpected place?

2. How can you make your home or workplace a **makom** of worship?

3. Do you recognize God's presence even in ordinary places?

Day 40: Yeshivah (יְשִׁיבָה)

- **Meaning:** Dwelling, Abiding

- **Bible Reference:** Psalm 91:1 – *"He who dwells (yeshivah) in the secret place of the Most High shall abide under the shadow of the Almighty."*

Message: Yeshivah describes not just visiting but dwelling with God. Many people seek God in crisis but do not remain in His presence. Jesus called His disciples to abide in Him, to stay connected like branches to a vine. Dwelling in God's presence transforms our hearts and minds. A life of abiding brings peace, strength, and wisdom. Are you dwelling or just visiting?

Reflection Questions for the Day:

1. What does it mean to truly abide in God?

2. How can you remain in His presence daily?

3. Do you pursue God consistently, or only in times of need?

Day 41: Asher (אָשֶׁר)

- **Meaning:** Blessed, Happy, Fulfilled

- **Bible Reference:** Psalm 1:1 – *"Blessed (asher) is the one who does not walk in step with the wicked."*

Message: Asher refers to a deep, lasting joy that comes from walking in God's ways. True blessing is not found in wealth or status but in being close to God. The Psalms describe the **asher** of those who meditate on His Word, trust in Him, and seek His presence. Jesus echoed this in the Beatitudes—true happiness is found in dependence on God. Are you seeking the right kind of blessing?

Reflection Questions for the Day:

1. What does true blessing look like in God's eyes?

2. Are you seeking happiness in temporary things or in God's presence?

3. How can you walk in the **asher** that comes from knowing Him?

Day 42: Anan (עֲנָן)

- **Meaning:** Cloud, Covering, Guidance

- **Bible Reference:** Exodus 13:21 – *"By day the Lord went ahead of them in a pillar of cloud (anan) to guide them on their way."*

Message: The **anan** was God's visible guidance for Israel in the wilderness. His presence led them, protected them, and showed them when to move and when to stay. Today, we are led by His Spirit, not by a cloud, but His guidance is just as real. When we follow Him, He directs our paths and provides clarity in uncertainty. Are you allowing God to guide your steps?

Reflection Questions for the Day:

1. How do you seek God's guidance in your life?

2. What steps can you take to trust His leading more?

3. Are you moving in your own direction or following God's path?

Week 6 Conclusion

This week, we explored powerful words that reveal different aspects of God's presence. His **Shekinah** fills the lives of those who seek Him, and His **kavod** carries the weight of His glory. Seeking His **panim** leads to deeper intimacy, and recognizing His **makom** reminds us that every place can be sacred. When we truly **yeshivah** (dwell) in His presence, we experience the true **asher** (blessed life) that comes from knowing Him. Like the **anan** that guided Israel, His Spirit leads us daily. As we reflect on these words, may we pursue

God's presence not just in moments of worship, but in every aspect of our lives.

Week 7: Trusting in God's Provision

Day 43: Manna (מָן)

- **Meaning:** What is it? (Bread from Heaven)

- **Bible Reference:** Exodus 16:15 – *"When the Israelites saw it, they said to each other, 'What is it?' (manna) For they did not know what it was."*

Message: God provided **manna** daily in the wilderness, teaching Israel to depend on Him. It was nourishment from heaven, reminding them that He was their provider. Jesus later declared that He is the true **manna**, the Bread of Life. God still provides for His people, but He often does so in unexpected ways. Trust in His daily provision, even when you don't fully understand His methods.

Reflection Questions for the Day:

1. How do you see God providing for you daily?

2. Are you trusting in Him or in your own efforts?

3. What does it mean for Jesus to be the Bread of Life?

Day 44: Yobel (יוֹבֵל)

- **Meaning:** Jubilee, Release, Freedom

- **Bible Reference:** Leviticus 25:10 – *"Consecrate the fiftieth year and proclaim liberty throughout the land to all its inhabitants. It shall be a jubilee (yobel) for you."*

Message: Yobel was a year of release—debts were forgiven, slaves were freed, and land was restored. It was a reminder that everything ultimately belongs to God. Jesus fulfilled the true **yobel**, setting us free from sin and bondage. God calls us to live in the freedom He provides, trusting that He is our

52

ultimate source of security. Are you living in the liberty of God's provision?

Reflection Questions for the Day:

1. What does spiritual freedom mean to you?

2. Are there any burdens you need to release to God?

3. How can you reflect God's provision to others in need?

Day 45: Shefa (שֶׁ פַ ע)

- **Meaning:** Abundance, Overflowing Blessing

- **Bible Reference:** Psalm 36:8 – *"They feast on the abundance (shefa) of Your house; You give them drink from Your river of delights."*

Message: God's **shefa** is more than just material wealth—it is His overflowing presence, joy, and peace. When we trust Him, we experience **shefa** in our spiritual and physical lives. True abundance comes from intimacy with God, not from earthly riches. Jesus promised an abundant life, but it is found in surrender to Him. Are you seeking God's abundance in the right places?

Reflection Questions for the Day:

1. How do you define abundance in your life?

2. Are you relying on God's blessings or chasing after worldly wealth?

3. How can you experience God's overflowing provision today?

Day 46: Betach (בֶּ טַ ח)

- **Meaning:** Trust, Security, Confidence

- **Bible Reference:** Proverbs 3:5 – *"Trust (betach) in the Lord with all your heart and lean not on your own understanding."*

Message: Betach is a deep, unwavering trust in God, the kind that brings true security. The world offers temporary safety, but only God provides lasting peace. Trusting in Him means surrendering control, even when we don't see the full picture. The more we rely on Him, the stronger our faith grows. Are you placing your trust in God or in temporary things?

Reflection Questions for the Day:

1. What does trusting God look like in your daily life?

2. Are there areas where you struggle to fully surrender to Him?

3. How can you build deeper confidence in God's provision?

Day 47: Goral (גּוֹרָל)

- **Meaning:** Lot, Portion, Destiny

- **Bible Reference:** Proverbs 16:33 – *"The lot (goral) is cast into the lap, but its every decision is from the Lord."*

Message: Goral was used in ancient times to determine outcomes, but ultimately, God controlled the results. Our lives are not determined by luck but by God's sovereign plan. When we trust in Him, we realize that every portion He gives is for our good. Instead of worrying about fate, we can rest in

His perfect will. Are you content with the portion God has given you?

Reflection Questions for the Day:

1. Do you trust that God is in control of your life's direction?

2. How do you respond when things don't go as planned?

3. What does it mean to accept your **goral** with faith?

Day 48: Machseh (מַ_חֲ_ס_ֶה)

- **Meaning:** Refuge, Shelter, Hiding Place

- **Bible Reference:** Psalm 91:2 – *"I will say of the Lord, 'He is my refuge (machseh) and my fortress, my God in whom I trust.'"*

Message: God is our **machseh**, a refuge in times of trouble. When life is uncertain, He is the unshakable place of safety. Running to Him is not weakness—it is wisdom. Jesus offers rest for the weary, inviting us to take shelter in Him. Are you seeking your refuge in God, or in temporary comforts?

Reflection Questions for the Day:

1. Where do you turn when life gets overwhelming?

2. How does trusting God as your refuge change your perspective on trials?

3. How can you help others find refuge in Him?

Day 49: Nachalah (נַ_חֲ_ל_ָה)

- **Meaning:** Inheritance, Possession, Heritage

- **Bible Reference:** Deuteronomy 4:20 – *"But as for you, the Lord took you and brought you out of the iron-smelting furnace, out of Egypt, to be the people of His inheritance (nachalah)."*

Message: Nachalah refers to the inheritance that God promised His people. Israel received a physical land, but believers today inherit the kingdom of God. Our greatest treasure is not earthly possessions but eternal life with Christ. When we trust in Him, we receive an inheritance that will never fade. Are you living with an eternal perspective?

Reflection Questions for the Day:

1. What does it mean to have an eternal inheritance?

2. How does knowing your spiritual **nachalah** change the way you live?

3. Are you investing in temporary things or in what will last forever?

Week 7 Conclusion

This week's words remind us that God provides for His people in ways both seen and unseen. He gave **manna** to Israel, teaching them daily dependence on Him. The concept of **yobel** shows that He desires freedom, not bondage, for His people. When we seek His **shefa**, we find true abundance— not in material wealth, but in His presence. **Betach** reminds us that trust is the foundation of provision; when we place our confidence in Him, we do not have to fear. Even when our **goral** seems uncertain, we can trust that God is in control. He is our **machseh**, a refuge in every storm, and He has promised us an eternal **nachalah**—a lasting inheritance beyond this life. May we walk in faith, knowing that our Heavenly Father supplies all our needs.

Week 8: The Power of God's Word

Day 50: Chokhmah (חָכְמָה)

- **Meaning:** Wisdom, Skill, Understanding

- **Bible Reference:** Proverbs 9:10 – *"The fear of the Lord is the beginning of wisdom (chokhmah), and the knowledge of the Holy One is understanding."*

Message: God's **chokhmah** is not just knowledge but skillful living aligned with His will. True wisdom begins with reverence for Him. Solomon sought **chokhmah**, and God granted him understanding beyond measure. Jesus embodies divine wisdom, and in Him, we find true insight. Do you seek earthly knowledge, or do you pursue godly **chokhmah**?

Reflection Questions for the Day:

1. How does wisdom differ from knowledge?

2. In what areas of your life do you need more **chokhmah**?

3. How can you grow in wisdom through God's Word?

Day 51: Pesher (פֶּשֶׁר)

- **Meaning:** Interpretation, Understanding of Scripture

- **Bible Reference:** Daniel 5:12 – *"Daniel was found to have a keen mind and knowledge and understanding, and also the ability to interpret (pesher) dreams, explain riddles, and solve difficult problems."*

Message: Pesher refers to understanding divine mysteries and interpreting Scripture correctly. Daniel had the ability to discern meanings beyond human wisdom. Jesus opened the eyes of His disciples to understand the Scriptures fully. The

Holy Spirit helps believers gain insight into God's Word. Are you seeking deeper understanding of His truth?

Reflection Questions for the Day:

1. How can you grow in interpreting and understanding the Bible?

2. What role does the Holy Spirit play in giving **pesher**?

3. Are you relying on your own interpretation or God's wisdom?

Day 52: Emet (אֱ‎מֶ‎ת)

- **Meaning:** Truth, Faithfulness, Firmness

- **Bible Reference:** Psalm 119:160 – *"The sum of Your word is truth (emet), and every one of Your righteous rules endures forever."*

Message: Emet means absolute truth, which is found in God alone. The world offers changing ideas, but His Word remains unshakable. Jesus declared that He is the truth, and knowing Him sets us free. Truth is not relative; it is anchored in God's character. Are you building your life on the **emet** of God's Word?

Reflection Questions for the Day:

1. How does God's truth differ from worldly perspectives?

2. Are there areas where you struggle to accept God's **emet**?

3. How can you live more fully in alignment with biblical truth?

Day 53: Sefer (סֵ פֶ ר)

- **Meaning:** Book, Scroll, Written Record

- **Bible Reference:** Joshua 1:8 – *"Keep this Book (sefer) of the Law always on your lips; meditate on it day and night."*

Message: The **sefer** of God's law is a written testimony of His will and commands. The Bible is more than literature—it is the living Word. God's instructions were written so His people could remember and obey them. Jesus fulfilled the **sefer**, embodying God's Word in the flesh. Do you cherish and meditate on His **sefer** daily?

Reflection Questions for the Day:

1. How does reading the Bible shape your daily life?

2. Do you meditate on God's Word or just read it?

3. What changes can you make to engage more with Scripture?

Day 54: Doresh (דּוֹ רֵ שׁ)

- **Meaning:** To Seek, To Study, To Inquire

- **Bible Reference:** Jeremiah 29:13 – *"You will seek (doresh) Me and find Me when you search for Me with all your heart."*

Message: Doresh is an active seeking of God and His Word. Studying Scripture requires intentional pursuit, not passive reading. Those who truly **doresh** the Lord will find Him. The Pharisees studied but missed the heart of God's Word. Are you seeking Him with an open heart?

Reflection Questions for the Day:

61

1. How intentional are you in studying God's Word?

2. What steps can you take to seek Him more earnestly?

3. Are you pursuing knowledge alone, or are you seeking a relationship with God?

Day 55: Mishpat (מִ שְׁ פָּ ט)

- **Meaning:** Judgment, Justice, Righteous Ruling

- **Bible Reference:** Deuteronomy 32:4 – *"All His ways are justice (mishpat); a God of faithfulness and without iniquity, just and upright is He."*

Message: Mishpat refers to God's righteous judgment and His just laws. He rules with perfect fairness, ensuring that justice prevails. While human justice is flawed, God's **mishpat** is true and unchanging. Jesus bore our judgment so that we could receive grace. Do you trust in God's **mishpat** rather than the world's system?

Reflection Questions for the Day:

1. How does God's justice differ from human justice?

2. Do you struggle to trust in His fairness?

3. How can you reflect God's justice in your daily life?

Day 56: Torah Ohr (תּוֹר ָ ה אוֹר)

- **Meaning:** Law of Light, Illuminating Word of God

- **Bible Reference:** Proverbs 6:23 – *"For the commandment is a lamp and the law (Torah Ohr) is light."*

Message: Torah Ohr signifies God's Word as a guiding light in darkness. Scripture provides direction, revealing truth and wisdom. Without His Word, we stumble, but His commands illuminate the path. Jesus, the Light of the World, fulfills and embodies **Torah Ohr**. Are you walking in the light of His truth?

Reflection Questions for the Day:

1. How does God's Word provide light in your life?

2. Are you walking in the guidance of His commandments?

3. What can you do to ensure His Word remains a lamp to your feet?

Week 8 Conclusion

This week's words highlight the significance of God's Word as the foundation of wisdom, understanding, and guidance. Seeking **chokhmah** leads to skillful living, while **pesher** helps us interpret Scripture rightly. God's **emet** remains unshaken despite cultural shifts, and His **sefer** (written Word) is preserved for our instruction. To truly grow, we must **doresh**—actively seek His truth—not just for knowledge but for transformation. His **mishpat** reminds us that His judgments are perfect and fair, guiding us in righteousness. The **Torah Ohr** is our light, showing us how to walk in His ways. May we continue to build our lives upon His Word, trusting that it leads us into truth and life.

Week 9: God's Strength in Times of Trouble

Day 57: Oz (עֹז)

- **Meaning:** Strength, Might, Power

- **Bible Reference:** Psalm 28:7 – *"The Lord is my strength (oz) and my shield; my heart trusts in Him, and He helps me."*

Message: God's **oz** is the source of all true strength. Human strength fades, but His power never fails. Throughout the Bible, people who relied on their own strength failed, but those who depended on God were victorious. David found strength in the Lord when facing enemies, and Paul declared that God's power is perfected in weakness. We may feel weak, but God's **oz** sustains us through every trial. His strength is not just for battle—it is for daily endurance, faithfulness, and perseverance. When we lean on Him, we are empowered to overcome challenges beyond our ability. Are you relying on your own strength or trusting in God's **oz**?

Reflection Questions for the Day:

1. In what areas of your life do you need God's strength?

2. How can you rely more on His power instead of your own?

3. What is one practical way you can trust in His **oz** today?

Day 58: Ma'oz (מָעֹוז)

- **Meaning:** Refuge, Stronghold, Defense

- **Bible Reference:** Nahum 1:7 – *"The Lord is good, a refuge (ma'oz) in times of trouble; He cares for those who trust in Him."*

Message: God is our **ma'oz**, a stronghold and place of safety. When life is chaotic, we can run to Him and find security. The world offers temporary refuge, but God's protection is eternal. The Israelites found safety in fortified cities, but true security came from trusting in the Lord. Jesus is our **ma'oz**, the rock that cannot be shaken. No enemy, trial, or fear is greater than His power to protect. Are you seeking shelter in temporary things, or are you trusting in God as your unshakable refuge?

Reflection Questions for the Day:

1. What does it mean to take refuge in God?

2. How can you turn to Him as your stronghold in difficult times?

3. Are there any fears you need to surrender to Him today?

Day 59: Tzur (צוּר)

- **Meaning:** Rock, Foundation, Strength

- **Bible Reference:** Deuteronomy 32:4 – *"He is the Rock (tzur), His works are perfect, and all His ways are just."*

Message: God is our **tzur**, the firm foundation that never moves. In ancient times, rocks symbolized stability and strength. Jesus used this imagery, saying that those who build their lives on Him will stand firm. The shifting sands of life cannot support us, but God's truth provides a firm place to stand. When everything around us is uncertain, His faithfulness remains. He is the unchanging rock in a changing world. Are you building your life on the solid rock or on things that crumble?

Reflection Questions for the Day:

1. What does it mean to build your life on God's firm foundation?

2. How has God been your **tzur** in difficult times?

3. Are you trusting in things that can shift, or in the unshakable Rock?

Day 60: Nissi (נִסִּי)

- **Meaning:** Banner, Victory, Standard

- **Bible Reference:** Exodus 17:15 – *"Moses built an altar and called it 'The Lord is my Banner (Yahweh-Nissi).'"*

Message: A **nissi** was a banner lifted high in battle, symbolizing victory and unity. When Israel fought against Amalek, they won as long as Moses held up his hands. Their victory came not from their strength but from God's power. Jesus is our **nissi**, the sign of our salvation and triumph over sin. When we face spiritual battles, we must remember that He has already won the victory. Keeping our eyes on Him gives us confidence and courage. Are you fighting in your own strength, or are you standing under God's banner of victory?

Reflection Questions for the Day:

1. What does it mean for God to be your **nissi**?

2. In what areas of life do you need His victory?

3. How can you keep your focus on His power rather than your struggles?

Day 61: Mish'en (מִשְׁעֵן)

- **Meaning:** Support, Stay, Upholder

- **Bible Reference:** Isaiah 41:10 – *"I will strengthen you and help you; I will uphold (mish'en) you with My righteous right hand."*

Message: God is our **mish'en**, the one who holds us up when we feel like falling. The burdens of life can be overwhelming, but He promises to sustain us. We often lean on people, finances, or plans, but these things can fail. Only God can truly support us in every season. His righteous hand lifts us when we are weak and carries us when we cannot walk. He is not just a temporary help—He is our eternal **mish'en**. Are you relying on things that cannot uphold you, or are you trusting in God's strength?

Reflection Questions for the Day:

1. What are you leaning on for support in your life?

2. How can you allow God to uphold you more fully?

3. What is one way you can strengthen your faith in His sustaining power?

Day 62: Gadal (גָּ דַ ל)

- **Meaning:** To Grow, Become Great, Magnify

- **Bible Reference:** Psalm 34:3 – *"Magnify (gadal) the Lord with me; let us exalt His name together."*

Message: To **gadal** is to magnify, to make great, or to grow. When we magnify God in our lives, our perspective shifts. Instead of focusing on our problems, we focus on His greatness. Worship enlarges our view of God, reminding us that He is bigger than anything we face. As we grow in faith, our trust in His power deepens. The more we **gadal** the Lord, the less fear controls us. Are you magnifying God, or are you magnifying your struggles?

Reflection Questions for the Day:

1. What does it mean to magnify God in your life?

2. How can focusing on His greatness help you through trials?

3. What steps can you take to grow in faith and trust?

Day 63: Chesuq (חֶ֫זֶק)

- **Meaning:** Firmness, Strengthening, Encouragement

- **Bible Reference:** 1 Samuel 30:6 – *"But David strengthened (chesuq) himself in the Lord his God."*

Message: Chesuq means to be strengthened, made firm, or encouraged. David strengthened himself in God when he faced despair. Life will bring moments of weakness, but God gives us the strength to persevere. Encouragement from His Word and His Spirit renews our strength. When we feel weary, He revives our faith. Strength does not always mean an escape from difficulty—it means endurance through it. Are you finding your encouragement in God or in temporary comforts?

Reflection Questions for the Day:

1. How do you strengthen yourself in the Lord?

2. Are you seeking encouragement from God or from unreliable sources?

3. How can you encourage someone else with God's strength today?

Week 9 Conclusion

This week's words remind us that our strength comes from God, not from ourselves. His **oz** gives us the power to stand firm, and He is our **ma'oz**, a refuge in times of trouble. When we feel unstable, He is our **tzur**, our solid foundation. Under His **nissi**, we find victory, knowing He fights for us. He upholds us as our **mish'en**, supporting us when we feel weak. As we **gadal** Him, our faith grows stronger, and through His **chesuq**, we are renewed. No matter what challenges arise, we can trust in the unshakable strength of our God.

Week 10: The Path of Righteousness

Day 64: Derekh (דֶּרֶךְ)

- **Meaning:** Way, Path, Journey

- **Bible Reference:** Proverbs 3:6 – *"In all your ways (derekh) acknowledge Him, and He will make your paths straight."*

Message: Derekh refers to the road we walk, both physically and spiritually. Throughout Scripture, God calls His people to walk in His **derekh**, the path of righteousness. Jesus described Himself as "the Way," emphasizing that following Him is not just about belief but a way of life. Many roads lead to destruction, but God's **derekh** leads to life. When we stray, He lovingly redirects us back. Walking in His way requires daily surrender, trust, and obedience. Are you following the path God has set before you?

Reflection Questions for the Day:

1. What does it mean to walk in God's **derekh**?

2. Are there any areas where you have strayed from His path?

3. How can you realign yourself with God's way today?

Day 65: Tsedeq (צֶדֶק)

- **Meaning:** Righteousness, Justice, Uprightness

- **Bible Reference:** Psalm 89:14 – *"Righteousness (tsedeq) and justice are the foundation of Your throne; love and faithfulness go before You."*

Message: God's **tsedeq** is His perfect righteousness, the standard by which all things are judged. Unlike human justice, which is often flawed, God's justice is true and fair.

72

He calls His people to live in **tsedeq**, reflecting His character in their actions. Jesus, the Righteous One, fulfilled God's **tsedeq**, making a way for us to be made right with Him. Living righteously is not about perfection but about surrendering to God's will. True righteousness flows from a transformed heart, not just outward actions. Are you pursuing God's righteousness in all areas of your life?

Reflection Questions for the Day:

1. How does God's **tsedeq** differ from worldly justice?

2. What areas of your life need more alignment with God's righteousness?

3. How can you reflect His justice and fairness in your daily actions?

Day 66: Yashar (יָשָׁר)

- **Meaning:** Upright, Straight, Honest

- **Bible Reference:** Proverbs 11:3 – *"The integrity of the upright (yashar) guides them, but the unfaithful are destroyed by their duplicity."*

Message: Yashar describes the quality of being upright, walking in honesty and truth. A person who is **yashar** does not compromise righteousness for personal gain. In a world filled with deception, God calls His people to integrity. The straight path is not always the easiest, but it is the way of blessing. Jesus lived with complete **yashar**, always speaking truth and acting with integrity. Those who walk uprightly will experience God's guidance and favor. Are you living a life of integrity in all that you do?

Reflection Questions for the Day:

1. What does it mean to be truly upright before God?

2. Are there any areas where you struggle with integrity?

3. How can you strengthen your commitment to honesty and righteousness?

Day 67: Tamim (תָּ מִ ים)

- **Meaning:** Blameless, Whole, Complete

- **Bible Reference:** Psalm 15:2 – *"The one whose walk is blameless (tamim), who does what is righteous, who speaks the truth from their heart."*

Message: Tamim signifies completeness and moral integrity. To be **tamim** does not mean being sinless, but rather being wholehearted in devotion to God. Throughout Scripture, God calls His people to walk blamelessly before Him. Noah was described as **tamim** in his generation, set apart by his obedience to God. Jesus was the ultimate **tamim**, the spotless Lamb of God. Living blamelessly means seeking God's will above all else, avoiding compromise and half-hearted devotion. Are you striving for wholehearted obedience in your walk with God?

Reflection Questions for the Day:

1. What does it mean to live a blameless life?

2. Are there areas where you struggle with divided devotion?

3. How can you pursue a more complete and wholehearted walk with God?

Day 68: Hesed (חֶ סֶ ד)

- **Meaning:** Lovingkindness, Faithful Love, Mercy

- **Bible Reference:** Micah 6:8 – *"What does the Lord require of you? To act justly, to love mercy (hesed), and to walk humbly with your God."*

Message: Hesed is God's faithful, covenantal love—a love that never fails. His mercy and kindness are not based on our actions but on His unchanging nature. Walking in righteousness means extending **hesed** to others, just as God extends it to us. Jesus embodied **hesed**, showing kindness to sinners, healing the broken, and forgiving those who betrayed Him. True righteousness is not just about rules but about love in action. Are you displaying God's **hesed** in your relationships?

Reflection Questions for the Day:

1. How have you experienced God's **hesed** in your life?

2. Are you extending lovingkindness to others, even when it's difficult?

3. What practical ways can you reflect God's mercy today?

Day 69: Tsaddiq (צַ ד יק)

- **Meaning:** Righteous Person, Just One

- **Bible Reference:** Proverbs 10:25 – *"When the storm has swept by, the wicked are gone, but the righteous (tsaddiq) stand firm forever."*

Message: A **tsaddiq** is one who walks in righteousness, living in obedience to God. The Bible contrasts the **tsaddiq** with the wicked, showing that the righteous will ultimately prevail. Jesus is the true **tsaddiq**, and through Him, we are made righteous before God. The world often opposes

75

righteousness, but God honors those who live according to His ways. The righteous are not perfect but are set apart by their faith and trust in God. Are you striving to live as a **tsaddiq** in a world that resists godliness?

Reflection Questions for the Day:

1. What qualities define a **tsaddiq** according to Scripture?

2. How can you grow in righteousness before God?

3. What challenges do you face in living a godly life, and how can you overcome them?

Day 70: Orakh (אֹ רַ ח)

- **Meaning:** Path, Way of Life, Conduct

- **Bible Reference:** Psalm 1:6 – *"For the Lord watches over the way (orakh) of the righteous, but the way of the wicked leads to destruction."*

Message: Orakh refers to a chosen way of life, a direction that shapes one's destiny. Every person walks a path—some lead to life, while others lead to destruction. The righteous walk in God's **orakh**, following His commands and seeking His presence. Jesus spoke of the narrow road that leads to life, a path that requires faith and commitment. God promises to guide those who seek Him on the right path. Are you walking in the **orakh** that leads to life?

Reflection Questions for the Day:

1. What path are you currently walking in your spiritual life?

2. How can you ensure you are following God's **orakh**?

3.   What steps can you take to stay on the right path?

Week 10 Conclusion

This week, we explored the journey of righteousness and what it means to walk in God's way. His **derekh** leads us toward His will, marked by **tsedeq**—true justice and righteousness. To live uprightly, we must cultivate **yashar**—integrity in all we do. Seeking to be **tamim**, blameless and complete before God, draws us closer to Him. At the heart of righteousness is **hesed**, a love that reflects God's mercy and faithfulness. Those who live as a **tsaddiq** will stand firm, rooted in His truth. Choosing the right **orakh** each day ensures that we remain on the narrow path that leads to life. May we commit ourselves daily to walking in righteousness, trusting in God's guidance every step of the way.

Week 11: The Power of Prayer and Seeking God

Day 71: Tefillah (תְּפִלָה)

- **Meaning:** Prayer, Petition, Intercession

- **Bible Reference:** Psalm 145:18 – *"The Lord is near to all who call on Him, to all who call on Him in truth."*

Message: Tefillah is not just a routine practice but an intimate conversation with God. In Scripture, we see prayer as a way of seeking guidance, expressing gratitude, and interceding for others. David, Daniel, and Jesus Himself demonstrated lives of consistent **tefillah**. Prayer is not about empty words but about aligning our hearts with God's will. When we call upon Him with sincerity, He hears and responds. The depth of our relationship with God is reflected in our **tefillah** life. Are you setting aside time daily to connect with God in prayer?

Reflection Questions for the Day:

1. How often do you engage in deep, intentional prayer?

2. In what areas of your life do you need to seek God more earnestly?

3. How can you make prayer a more central part of your daily routine?

Day 72: Hineni (הִנֵנִי)

- **Meaning:** Here I am, Availability to God

- **Bible Reference:** Isaiah 6:8 – *"Then I heard the voice of the Lord saying, 'Whom shall I send? And who will go for us?' And I said, 'Here am I (hineni). Send me!'"*

Message: Hineni is a response of total availability to God. When God called Abraham, Moses, and Isaiah, they answered with **hineni**, expressing their readiness to obey. True prayer is not only speaking to God but also listening and responding. Saying **hineni** means surrendering our plans and being willing to follow His leading. It is a declaration of faith, trust, and willingness to serve. God is always calling—are you ready to say, "Here I am"?

Reflection Questions for the Day:

1. Are you fully available for God's call in your life?

2. What holds you back from saying **hineni** to God?

3. How can you cultivate a heart that is always ready to serve Him?

Day 73: Qara (קָ,ר,א)

- **Meaning:** To Call, Cry Out, Proclaim

- **Bible Reference:** Jeremiah 33:3 – *"Call (qara) to Me and I will answer you and tell you great and unsearchable things you do not know."*

Message: God invites us to **qara**, to call upon Him with boldness and expectation. Throughout Scripture, people cried out to God in times of distress, repentance, and worship. He promises to hear and respond to those who seek Him. **Qara** is not a passive whisper but an active, faith-filled cry. It is an act of trust, believing that God is near and willing to move in our lives. When we call upon Him, we open ourselves to His wisdom and power. Are you calling on God with confidence and expectation?

Reflection Questions for the Day:

1. When was the last time you called out to God with urgency?

2. How does God's promise to answer encourage you to pray more boldly?

3. What is stopping you from calling on God for help right now?

Day 74: Chanan (חָנַן)

- **Meaning:** To Be Gracious, Show Favor

- **Bible Reference:** Numbers 6:25 – *"The Lord make His face shine on you and be gracious (chanan) to you."*

Message: God is full of **chanan**, grace, and favor toward His people. We do not earn His mercy—it is freely given through His love. The Psalms are filled with prayers asking for God's **chanan**, seeking His kindness and blessings. Jesus, through His sacrifice, is the greatest expression of God's grace. When we pray, we come before a gracious God who delights in showing mercy. Because we have received His grace, we are also called to extend **chanan** to others. Are you living in the awareness of God's grace and extending it to those around you?

Reflection Questions for the Day:

1. How have you experienced God's grace in your life?

2. Do you approach prayer with the confidence that God is gracious?

3. How can you show more grace to others as God has shown it to you?

Day 75: Shavat (שָׁ_בַ_ת)

- **Meaning:** To Rest, Cease, Be Still

- **Bible Reference:** Psalm 46:10 – *"Be still (shavat) and know that I am God."*

Message: In a fast-paced world, we often struggle to **shavat**, to pause and rest in God's presence. Prayer is not just about speaking—it also involves silence and listening. Jesus often withdrew to quiet places to pray, modeling the importance of stillness before God. When we cease striving, we make space for God to work in our hearts. **Shavat** reminds us that God is in control, and we don't have to carry everything alone. Resting in Him renews our strength and deepens our faith. Are you taking time to be still and listen to God?

Reflection Questions for the Day:

1. How often do you take time to be still in God's presence?

2. What distractions keep you from resting in Him?

3. How can practicing **shavat** strengthen your faith?

Day 76: Bakash (בָּ_קַ_שׁ)

- **Meaning:** To Seek, Search, Desire Earnestly

- **Bible Reference:** Matthew 7:7 – *"Ask, and it will be given to you; seek (bakash), and you will find; knock, and it will be opened to you."*

Message: Bakash is more than a casual search—it is an intense pursuit of God's presence and will. Seeking God requires diligence, consistency, and a heart that longs for Him above all else. The Bible promises that those who seek Him will find Him. Jesus encouraged His followers to keep asking, seeking, and knocking, showing that persistent faith leads to deeper encounters with God. True prayer is fueled by a heart that is always searching for more of Him. Are you passionately seeking God in your prayers and daily life?

Reflection Questions for the Day:

1. What does it mean to seek God with all your heart?

2. How can you be more intentional about pursuing Him daily?

3. What steps can you take to deepen your spiritual hunger for God?

Day 77: Paga (פָ גַ עַ)

- **Meaning:** To Intercede, Meet, Encounter

- **Bible Reference:** Isaiah 53:12 – *"He bore the sin of many and made intercession (paga) for the transgressors."*

Message: Paga means to intercede, to stand in the gap between God and others. Jesus is the ultimate intercessor, praying on our behalf even now. Intercessory prayer is a calling to pray for others, lifting their burdens before the Lord. When we **paga**, we align with God's heart and become part of His work in people's lives. Abraham interceded for Sodom, Moses for Israel, and the church is called to intercede for the world. True prayer is not just about our needs but about standing in the gap for others. Are you making time to intercede for those around you?

Reflection Questions for the Day:

1. Who in your life needs intercessory prayer right now?

2. How can you grow in your commitment to praying for others?

3. What does it mean to be an intercessor in God's kingdom?

Week 11 Conclusion

This week, we explored different aspects of prayer and how it connects us with God. **Tefillah** teaches us that prayer is an ongoing conversation, while **hineni** reminds us to be available for God's call. **Qara** challenges us to cry out boldly to Him, knowing that He listens. We are sustained by His **chanan**, His grace, which invites us to approach Him with confidence. **Shavat** calls us to rest and listen, allowing space for God to speak. As we **bakash**, we actively seek His presence and truth, and through **paga**, we intercede for others. Prayer is not just a ritual—it is the heartbeat of a relationship with God. May we continue to grow in our prayer lives, drawing closer to Him daily.

Week 12: The Power of God's Promises

Day 78: Dabar (דָּ֫בָ֫ר)

- **Meaning:** Word, Promise, Matter

- **Bible Reference:** Isaiah 40:8 – *"The grass withers, the flower fades, but the word (dabar) of our God will stand forever."*

Message: Dabar is not just speech; it is a word that carries weight, action, and power. When God speaks, His **dabar** does not return void—it accomplishes what He intends. Throughout Scripture, God makes promises, and His **dabar** is always fulfilled. His Word is eternal and unshakable, a foundation for our faith. Jesus is the living **dabar**, the Word made flesh, revealing God's faithfulness. When life feels uncertain, we can trust in the unchanging promises of God. Are you building your faith on His **dabar**, or are you relying on fleeting things?

Reflection Questions for the Day:

1. How do you view the promises of God in your life?

2. Are you trusting in His **dabar**, even when circumstances seem difficult?

3. What steps can you take to build your life on God's unshakable Word?

Day 79: Brit (בְּ֫רִ֫ית)

- **Meaning:** Covenant, Agreement, Promise

- **Bible Reference:** Genesis 17:7 – *"I will establish My covenant (brit) as an everlasting covenant between Me and you and your descendants after you."*

Message: A **brit** is a sacred agreement, an unbreakable bond between God and His people. In the Old Testament, God made covenants with Noah, Abraham, and Moses, always remaining faithful to His **brit** despite human failure. Jesus established a new **brit** through His blood, offering salvation and eternal life to all who believe. This covenant is based on God's grace, not our works. Trusting in God's **brit** means we live with confidence, knowing He will never abandon us. Are you living as someone who is secure in God's eternal covenant?

Reflection Questions for the Day:

1. What does it mean to be part of God's **brit**?

2. How does knowing that God keeps His promises affect your faith?

3. Are you living in a way that reflects the covenant relationship you have with God?

Day 80: Emunah (אֱמוּנָה)

- **Meaning:** Faith, Faithfulness, Steadfastness

- **Bible Reference:** Habakkuk 2:4 – *"The righteous shall live by his faith (emunah)."*

Message: **Emunah** is not just belief—it is steadfast faithfulness. It is the kind of trust that remains firm even when we don't see immediate answers. Abraham demonstrated **emunah** by believing in God's promise despite his old age. Jesus taught that faith as small as a mustard seed can move mountains. When we stand on God's promises, we exercise **emunah**, knowing that He is faithful even when circumstances challenge us. True **emunah** leads to action—

living in obedience because we trust God completely. Are you walking by faith or by sight?

Reflection Questions for the Day:

1. How does your faith influence your daily actions?

2. What challenges have tested your **emunah**, and how did you respond?

3. How can you grow in trusting God's promises more deeply?

Day 81: Yachal (יָחַל)

- **Meaning:** Hope, Waiting Expectantly

- **Bible Reference:** Psalm 130:5 – *"I wait for the Lord, my soul waits, and in His word I put my hope (yachal)."*

Message: Yachal means to wait with hope, trusting that God will fulfill His promises. Waiting is difficult, but when we wait with faith, we acknowledge that God's timing is perfect. Throughout Scripture, God's people had to **yachal**— Abraham waited for a son, Israel waited for deliverance, and we wait for Christ's return. Hope is not passive—it actively trusts that God is working even when we don't see immediate results. Jesus is our ultimate **yachal**, our sure and steadfast hope. Are you waiting with expectation or with doubt?

Reflection Questions for the Day:

1. How do you respond when God's promises seem delayed?

2. What is one way you can strengthen your hope in the Lord?

3. How does Jesus fulfill the deepest hope of your heart?

Day 82: Ne'eman (נֶ.אֱ.מָ.ן)

- **Meaning:** Faithful, Trustworthy, Reliable

- **Bible Reference:** Deuteronomy 7:9 – *"Know therefore that the Lord your God is God, the faithful (ne'eman) God, keeping His covenant of love to a thousand generations."*

Message: God is **ne'eman**—completely faithful, never failing in His promises. Unlike humans, who can be unreliable, God remains steadfast. When we struggle to trust, we can look back at His past faithfulness. His faithfulness is evident in history, in Scripture, and in our personal lives. Even when we are unfaithful, He remains **ne'eman**, calling us back to Him. Knowing that God is trustworthy gives us peace in every situation. Are you fully relying on His faithfulness?

Reflection Questions for the Day:

1. How has God shown His faithfulness in your life?

2. Are there areas where you struggle to trust that He is **ne'eman**?

3. How can remembering God's faithfulness give you confidence for the future?

Day 83: Shalom (שָׁ.לוֹם)

- **Meaning:** Peace, Wholeness, Completion

- **Bible Reference:** Isaiah 26:3 – *"You will keep in perfect peace (shalom) those whose minds are steadfast, because they trust in You."*

Message: Shalom is more than just peace—it is wholeness, harmony, and the fulfillment of God's promises. True **shalom** is found in trusting God's plans rather than striving in our own strength. Jesus is the Prince of **Shalom**, offering peace that surpasses understanding. When we believe in God's promises, we can experience **shalom** even in uncertainty. A heart rooted in God's Word will not be shaken by external circumstances. Are you living in the peace that comes from trusting in God's promises?

Reflection Questions for the Day:

1. What is stealing your peace right now?

2. How does trusting in God's promises bring true **shalom**?

3. How can you be a carrier of **shalom** to those around you?

Day 84: Go'el (גּוֹאֵל)

- **Meaning:** Redeemer, One Who Saves

- **Bible Reference:** Job 19:25 – *"I know that my Redeemer (go'el) lives, and that in the end He will stand on the earth."*

Message: A **go'el** is a redeemer, one who rescues and restores. In the Old Testament, a **go'el** would redeem family members from slavery or loss. Jesus is our ultimate **go'el**, purchasing our freedom from sin with His blood. Redemption is not just about being saved—it is about being restored to our original purpose in God. Because we are redeemed, we can walk in confidence, knowing that we belong to Him. His redemption is complete, covering every failure and securing our eternal future. Are you living as someone who has been redeemed?

Reflection Questions for the Day:

1. What does it mean for Jesus to be your **go'el**?

2. How has God's redemption transformed your life?

3. Are you living in the freedom that comes with being redeemed?

Week 12 Conclusion

This week's words remind us that God's promises are unshakable. His **dabar** is eternal, and His **brit** is an everlasting covenant that never fails. We are called to walk in **emunah**, a faith that trusts in His word, and to **yachal**, waiting with hope for His perfect timing. Because God is **ne'eman**, we can rely on Him completely, knowing that He will never abandon us. His promises bring **shalom**, a deep peace that goes beyond circumstances. As our **go'el**, He redeems and restores, proving His love through Christ's sacrifice. May we hold fast to His promises, walking daily in faith and trust.

Week 13: Walking in God's Wisdom

Day 85: Binah (בִּ.ינ.ה)

- **Meaning:** Understanding, Discernment, Insight

- **Bible Reference:** Proverbs 2:3 – *"Indeed, if you call out for insight (binah) and cry aloud for understanding."*

Message: Binah refers to a deep level of understanding that goes beyond knowledge. It is the ability to discern truth from falsehood and to perceive the heart of a matter. Throughout Scripture, wisdom and **binah** are gifts from God, given to those who seek Him. Solomon prayed for **binah**, knowing that ruling wisely required divine insight. The Holy Spirit grants believers spiritual **binah**, helping us navigate life with godly perspective. When we face difficult choices, seeking God's **binah** leads us to the right path. Are you relying on your own understanding, or are you asking God for **binah** in your decisions?

Reflection Questions for the Day:

1. What areas in your life require deeper understanding from God?

2. How can you develop discernment through prayer and Scripture?

3. Are you making decisions based on your knowledge or seeking divine **binah**?

Day 86: Da'at (דּ.ע.ת)

- **Meaning:** Knowledge, Perception, Awareness

- **Bible Reference:** Proverbs 1:7 – *"The fear of the Lord is the beginning of knowledge (da'at), but fools despise wisdom and instruction."*

Message: Da'at refers to knowledge that comes from God rather than human wisdom. The world offers knowledge, but without God, it is incomplete. True **da'at** starts with the fear of the Lord—a heart that reveres and honors Him. Knowing about God is not the same as knowing Him personally. The Bible teaches that seeking **da'at** leads to wisdom, but rejecting it leads to destruction. Jesus, the source of all truth, invites us to grow in knowledge of Him. Are you pursuing a deeper **da'at** of God, or are you content with surface-level faith?

Reflection Questions for the Day:

1. How does godly knowledge differ from worldly knowledge?

2. In what ways are you growing in your **da'at** of God?

3. How can you use your knowledge to strengthen your faith and help others?

Day 87: Sekhel (שֶׂ כֶ ל)

- **Meaning:** Prudence, Wisdom, Good Sense

- **Bible Reference:** 1 Samuel 25:3 – *"Abigail was an intelligent (sekhel) and beautiful woman, but her husband was harsh and evil in his dealings."*

Message: Sekhel is practical wisdom—the ability to make wise decisions in everyday life. Abigail demonstrated **sekhel** when she intervened to prevent David from making a rash decision. While knowledge is important, applying it with **sekhel** ensures that we act with wisdom. Many people have intelligence but lack wisdom in how they apply it. God calls us to walk with **sekhel**, thinking carefully before speaking or acting. The Holy Spirit provides wisdom to those who seek

Him. Are you exercising **sekhel** in your daily life, or do you act impulsively?

Reflection Questions for the Day:

1. How can you develop more prudence in your daily decisions?

2. Do you seek God's guidance before making important choices?

3. How can you apply wisdom in handling relationships and challenges?

Day 88: Ormah (עׇרְמׇה)

- **Meaning:** Shrewdness, Cunning, Strategic Thinking

- **Bible Reference:** Proverbs 8:12 – *"I, wisdom, dwell together with prudence (ormah); I possess knowledge and discretion."*

Message: Ormah is often translated as prudence, but it also implies strategic wisdom. While shrewdness can be used for evil, Godly **ormah** helps believers navigate life with discernment. Jesus told His followers to be "wise as serpents and innocent as doves," highlighting the need for both wisdom and purity. Nehemiah demonstrated **ormah** when rebuilding Jerusalem's walls, anticipating opposition and planning wisely. Christians must balance being innocent with being wise, knowing how to respond to challenges strategically. Walking with **ormah** means being alert to the schemes of the enemy while remaining faithful to God. Are you using wisdom to navigate challenges, or are you reacting without thought?

Reflection Questions for the Day:

1. How can strategic wisdom help you in your faith journey?

2. Are you balancing innocence with shrewdness in a godly way?

3. What steps can you take to grow in biblical **ormah**?

Day 89: Tushiyyah (תּוּשִׁיָּה)

- **Meaning:** Sound Wisdom, Resourcefulness, Sound Judgment

- **Bible Reference:** Job 12:13 – *"To God belong wisdom and power; counsel and understanding (tushiyyah) are His."*

Message: **Tushiyyah** represents wisdom that leads to success and stability. It is wisdom with depth—insight that goes beyond mere knowledge. In difficult situations, God provides **tushiyyah** to those who seek Him. Joseph displayed **tushiyyah** when interpreting Pharaoh's dreams and preparing for famine. The Bible encourages believers to pursue **tushiyyah,** seeking wisdom that brings peace and stability. This wisdom is not just for personal success but for guiding others in truth. Are you cultivating **tushiyyah** in your life, seeking wisdom that leads to lasting success?

Reflection Questions for the Day:

1. What is the difference between knowledge and sound wisdom?

2. How can you seek God's wisdom in making life choices?

3. Are you using your wisdom to help others find stability and peace?

Day 90: Mezimah (מְ זִ מָ ה)

- **Meaning:** Discretion, Purposeful Planning, Thoughtfulness

- **Bible Reference:** Proverbs 2:11 – *"Discretion (mezimah) will protect you, and understanding will guard you."*

Message: Mezimah is the ability to plan wisely, making thoughtful and intentional decisions. Godly discretion prevents foolish choices and protects from harm. Many people act on impulse, but **mezimah** considers the consequences before taking action. Proverbs teaches that **mezimah** guards us, leading us toward righteousness. Jesus demonstrated **mezimah** in His ministry, knowing when to speak, when to be silent, and when to withdraw. The wise person considers their words and actions carefully. Are you exercising discretion in your decisions, or are you acting without thinking?

Reflection Questions for the Day:

1. How can practicing discretion protect you from making mistakes?

2. Are there areas in your life where you need to be more thoughtful?

3. How can **mezimah** help you navigate relationships and responsibilities?

Day 91: Sachal (שָׂ כַ ל)

- **Meaning:** To Be Wise, Insightful, Successful

- **Bible Reference:** Joshua 1:8 – *"Keep this Book of the Law always on your lips; meditate on it day and*

97

night, so that you may be careful to do everything written in it. Then you will be prosperous and successful (sachal)."

Message: Sachal describes wisdom that leads to success in God's eyes. Joshua was promised success if he followed God's commands with diligence. Biblical success is not about wealth or power but about walking in obedience to God. True **sachal** brings fulfillment, peace, and purpose. It requires meditation on God's Word and application of His truth. Jesus lived with perfect **sachal**, fulfilling His mission with wisdom and insight. Are you pursuing success as the world defines it, or are you seeking godly wisdom that leads to lasting fulfillment?

Reflection Questions for the Day:

1. How does biblical success differ from worldly success?

2. Are you pursuing God's wisdom as the foundation for success?

3. How can meditating on God's Word lead to wise and successful living?

Week 13 Conclusion

This week, we explored different aspects of wisdom that help us walk in God's ways. **Binah** gives us deep discernment, while **da'at** reminds us that true knowledge begins with God. **Sekhel** helps us make wise daily decisions, and **ormah** teaches us strategic thinking. **Tushiyyah** leads to stability, guiding us toward choices that honor God. **Mezimah** encourages discretion in planning, protecting us from harmful decisions. Finally, **sachal** shows that true success is found in obedience to God.

Week 14: The Power of the Tongue and Our Words

Day 92: Lashon (לָשׁוֹן)

- **Meaning:** Tongue, Speech, Language

- **Bible Reference:** Proverbs 18:21 – *"The tongue (lashon) has the power of life and death, and those who love it will eat its fruit."*

Message: Our **lashon** (tongue) has the ability to bring life or destruction. Words can uplift, encourage, and heal, or they can wound and tear down. Scripture warns about the dangers of a reckless tongue—gossip, slander, and lies can ruin relationships and reputations. Jesus taught that what comes from our mouths reflects what is in our hearts. The wise person guards their **lashon**, speaking only what is true and edifying. When we surrender our words to God, our speech can be a source of grace and wisdom. Are you using your **lashon** to bring life, or are your words causing harm?

Reflection Questions for the Day:

1. How do your words impact those around you?

2. Are there areas where you need to be more careful with your speech?

3. How can you use your words to bring encouragement and truth?

Day 93: Peh (פֶּה)

- **Meaning:** Mouth, Speech, Declaration

- **Bible Reference:** Exodus 4:12 – *"Now go; I will help you speak (peh) and will teach you what to say."*

Message: The **peh** (mouth) is a tool that can be used for both good and evil. Moses felt inadequate to speak, but God assured him that He would give him the words. Often, we hesitate to speak truth because of fear or insecurity. However, when God calls us to speak, He equips us with the right words. The Bible reminds us to be slow to speak and quick to listen, ensuring that our words align with His will. Whether in prayer, teaching, or daily conversations, our **peh** should be used for God's glory. Are you allowing God to guide your speech?

Reflection Questions for the Day:

1. How do you use your **peh**—to bless or to harm?

2. Do you trust God to give you the right words when needed?

3. How can you be more intentional in using your mouth for good?

Day 94: Dibbūr (דִּבּוּר)

- **Meaning:** Speech, Utterance, Communication

- **Bible Reference:** Psalm 19:14 – *"May these words (dibbūr) of my mouth and this meditation of my heart be pleasing in Your sight, Lord, my Rock and my Redeemer."*

Message: Dibbūr refers to the act of speaking and the words we choose to communicate. The Bible places great emphasis on using our speech to glorify God. Harsh words stir up anger, while gentle words bring peace. Gossip and falsehoods destroy, but truth and wisdom build up. Jesus said that we will be judged for every careless word we speak. Therefore, we must train ourselves to speak words that align with His truth. Are your **dibbūr** bringing life and encouragement, or are they causing harm?

Reflection Questions for the Day:

1. How can you ensure your words are pleasing to God?

2. What are some harmful speech habits you need to change?

3. How can you use your words to bring healing and encouragement?

Day 95: Sheqer (שֶׁ֫קֶר)

- **Meaning:** Falsehood, Deception, Lying

- **Bible Reference:** Proverbs 12:22 – *"The Lord detests lying lips, but He delights in people who are trustworthy."*

Message: Sheqer refers to deceit and falsehood, something that the Bible strongly condemns. God is a God of truth, and lying is the opposite of His nature. Satan is called the "father of lies," showing that deception originates from sin. Lies may seem small or harmless, but they erode trust and damage relationships. Scripture teaches that those who walk in truth reflect the character of God. Speaking the truth, even when difficult, brings freedom and integrity. Are you committed to truthfulness in your speech and actions?

Reflection Questions for the Day:

1. Are there any areas where you struggle with truthfulness?

2. How can you resist the temptation to speak **sheqer**?

3. Why is honesty essential in your relationship with God and others?

Day 96: Emet (אֱמֶת)

- **Meaning:** Truth, Faithfulness, Firmness

- **Bible Reference:** Zechariah 8:16 – *"These are the things you are to do: Speak the truth (emet) to each other, and render true and sound judgment in your courts."*

Message: Emet is more than just telling the truth—it represents faithfulness and reliability. God's nature is **emet**, and He calls His people to walk in truth. Lies create division and instability, but **emet** builds trust and security. Jesus declared Himself to be "the way, the truth, and the life," showing that truth is central to our faith. As followers of Christ, we are called to live in **emet**, speaking and acting with integrity. Our commitment to truth should be unwavering, even when it is difficult. Are you reflecting God's **emet** in the way you speak and live?

Reflection Questions for the Day:

1. How does your life reflect God's **emet**?

2. What areas in your speech need more alignment with truth?

3. How can you be a stronger witness of God's truth to others?

Day 97: Nevuah (נְבוּאָה)

- **Meaning:** Prophecy, Divine Revelation

- **Bible Reference:** Amos 3:7 – *"Surely the Sovereign Lord does nothing without revealing His plan to His servants the prophets."*

Message: Nevuah is the word of God spoken through His chosen messengers. Prophets in the Bible were called to speak truth, warn of judgment, and reveal God's plans. While prophecy in Scripture is unique, the principle of speaking God's truth remains relevant today. The Holy Spirit equips believers to share His Word boldly. We may not all be prophets, but we are called to share the good news. Our words should align with God's truth, leading others to Him. Are you using your voice to proclaim God's truth?

Reflection Questions for the Day:

1. How can you be more intentional in speaking God's truth?

2. What role does prophecy play in your understanding of Scripture?

3. How can you be a messenger of hope and truth to others?

Day 98: Tehillah (תְּהִלָּה)

- **Meaning:** Praise, Song, Worshipful Speech

- **Bible Reference:** Psalm 34:1 – *"I will bless the Lord at all times; His praise (tehillah) will always be on my lips."*

Message: Tehillah is a form of worshipful speech, where words are used to praise God. The Psalms are filled with **tehillah**, showing that our words should glorify Him. When we praise, we shift our focus from problems to God's greatness. **Tehillah** is not just about music—it is about a heart that continually honors God with its speech. Complaining and negativity hinder worship, but thanksgiving and praise bring joy. Even in trials, we can offer **tehillah**, declaring that God is good. Are your words filled with praise or complaints?

Reflection Questions for the Day:

1. How often do you use your words to praise God?

2. How can **tehillah** change your perspective in difficult times?

3. What steps can you take to make praise a habit?

Week 14 Conclusion

This week's study reveals the incredible power our words hold. **Lashon** and **peh** remind us that our speech can bring life or destruction. **Dibbūr** shows that what we say should reflect God's truth, while **sheqer** warns us against deception. **Emet** calls us to walk in truth, just as Jesus did. **Nevuah** encourages us to proclaim God's Word, and **tehillah** reminds us that our speech should be filled with praise. Every word we speak has an impact—on ourselves, on others, and on our relationship with God. May we use our tongues wisely, speaking words that honor Him and bring life to those around us.

Week 15: The Heart's Condition and Spiritual Transformation

Day 99: Lev (לֵב)

- **Meaning:** Heart, Inner Being, Mind

- **Bible Reference:** Proverbs 4:23 – *"Above all else, guard your heart (lev), for everything you do flows from it."*

Message: The **lev** represents more than just the physical heart—it is the center of thoughts, emotions, and will. Throughout Scripture, God emphasizes the importance of a pure **lev** because it determines the course of life. Jesus taught that evil actions originate from a corrupted heart, but a heart surrendered to God produces righteousness. David prayed for a clean **lev**, knowing that transformation begins internally. True faith is not just about external obedience but a heart fully devoted to God. The condition of your **lev** affects your relationship with God and others. Are you guarding your heart, ensuring it is aligned with God's truth?

Reflection Questions for the Day:

1. What influences are shaping your heart daily?

2. How can you guard your heart from negative influences?

3. In what areas do you need a heart transformation?

Day 100: Ruach (רוּחַ)

- **Meaning:** Spirit, Breath, Wind

- **Bible Reference:** Ezekiel 36:26 – *"I will give you a new heart and put a new spirit (ruach) in you."*

Message: Ruach signifies the breath of God, His Spirit that brings life and renewal. When God created Adam, He breathed His **ruach** into him, giving him life. Similarly, when we come to Christ, the Holy Spirit regenerates our hearts, transforming us from within. Without God's **ruach**, we are spiritually dead, but with His Spirit, we are made alive. Ezekiel's vision of dry bones coming to life illustrates the power of God's **ruach** to restore and renew. The Holy Spirit guides, convicts, and strengthens believers, shaping them into the image of Christ. Are you allowing God's **ruach** to transform you daily?

Reflection Questions for the Day:

1. How have you experienced the Holy Spirit's work in your life?

2. Are you actively allowing the Holy Spirit to lead you?

3. What areas in your life need the refreshing breath of God?

Day 101: Nefesh (נֶפֶשׁ)

- **Meaning:** Soul, Life, Being

- **Bible Reference:** Psalm 42:2 – *"My soul (nefesh) thirsts for God, for the living God."*

Message: The **nefesh** is the essence of life—the soul that longs for connection with its Creator. David expressed deep longing for God, showing that our **nefesh** is only truly satisfied in Him. Many seek fulfillment in temporary things, but true satisfaction comes from spiritual intimacy with God. Jesus invites us to find rest for our **nefesh**, offering peace that the world cannot give. The health of our **nefesh** determines our spiritual well-being. When we nourish our soul with God's presence, we experience joy and fulfillment. Is your **nefesh** seeking after God, or is it restless and distracted?

Reflection Questions for the Day:

1. What are you feeding your soul with daily?

2. How can you cultivate a deeper longing for God?

3. Are you finding rest for your **nefesh**, or are you spiritually exhausted?

Day 102: Teshuvah (תְּשׁוּבָה)

- **Meaning:** Repentance, Return, Turning Back

- **Bible Reference:** Joel 2:13 – *"Return (teshuvah) to the Lord your God, for He is gracious and compassionate."*

Message: Teshuvah is more than just saying "I'm sorry"—it is a complete turning back to God. Repentance involves a change of heart, mind, and direction. Throughout the Bible, God calls His people to **teshuvah**, offering forgiveness and restoration. Jesus preached repentance, urging people to turn from sin and embrace the Kingdom of God. Genuine **teshuvah** brings freedom, as we are no longer bound by guilt and sin. God's mercy is always available, but we must be willing to turn back to Him. Are you walking in repentance, keeping your heart aligned with God?

Reflection Questions for the Day:

1. What areas in your life require true repentance?

2. Do you see **teshuvah** as a burden or a gift?

3. How does repentance bring spiritual renewal and freedom?

Day 103: Tahor (טָהוֹר)

- **Meaning:** Pure, Clean, Unblemished

- **Bible Reference:** Psalm 51:10 – *"Create in me a pure (tahor) heart, O God, and renew a steadfast spirit within me."*

Message: Tahor describes a state of purity, free from defilement. In the Old Testament, ceremonial purity was required for worship, but Jesus taught that true purity comes from the heart. A **tahor** heart is one that is undivided in its devotion to God. Sin corrupts, but through Christ, we are washed clean and made new. Pursuing purity is not just about avoiding sin but about desiring holiness. The Holy Spirit helps us maintain a **tahor** heart, shaping us into Christ's image. Are you striving for purity in your thoughts, actions, and desires?

Reflection Questions for the Day:

1. How can you cultivate a pure heart before God?

2. Are there any areas where you need cleansing?

3. How does purity bring you closer to God?

Day 104: Lev Chadash (לֵ ב חָ דָ שׁ)

- **Meaning:** New Heart, Transformed Heart

- **Bible Reference:** Ezekiel 11:19 – *"I will give them an undivided heart and put a new spirit in them."*

Message: God promises to give His people a **lev chadash**, a heart that is completely transformed. A new heart means new desires, new attitudes, and a renewed love for God. Transformation is not just about behavior but about a deep, inward change. Jesus spoke of being "born again," emphasizing the need for spiritual renewal. A **lev chadash** is free from hardness, open to God's leading, and full of His love. Only through Christ can our hearts be truly renewed. Do you have a **lev chadash**, or is your heart still hardened?

Reflection Questions for the Day:

1. What evidence of a **lev chadash** is seen in your life?

2. Are you resisting or embracing God's transformation?

3. How can you continue to grow in spiritual renewal?

Day 105: Lev Shalem (לֵב שָׁלֵם)

- **Meaning:** Wholehearted, Undivided Heart, Complete Devotion

- **Bible Reference:** 1 Kings 8:61 – *"Let your hearts (lev shalem) be fully committed to the Lord our God."*

Message: A **lev shalem** is a heart that is wholly devoted to God, without distraction or compromise. Many people struggle with divided hearts, torn between worldly desires and God's will. Throughout Scripture, God calls His people to serve Him with a **lev shalem**. Jesus taught that we cannot serve two masters; we must choose wholehearted devotion. When our hearts are fully committed, we experience the fullness of His presence and purpose. The more we surrender, the more we grow in faith and intimacy with God. Is your heart divided, or are you pursuing God with a **lev shalem**?

Reflection Questions for the Day:

1. What distractions pull your heart away from full devotion to God?

2. How can you cultivate a **lev shalem** in your daily walk?

3. What steps can you take to surrender more fully to God?

Week 15 Conclusion

This week's words reveal the journey of transformation that God desires for each of us. **Lev** reminds us that everything flows from the heart, making its condition vital. Through the power of God's **ruach**, we are renewed and given life. Our **nefesh** longs for intimacy with God, but we must respond with **teshuvah**, turning back to Him in repentance. A **tahor** heart seeks purity, and through Christ, we are given a **lev chadash**, a new heart. However, true transformation is not complete without a **lev shalem**, a heart fully devoted to God. As we examine our hearts, may we allow God to mold us, cleanse us, and make us whole.

Week 16: The Presence of God in Our Lives

Day 106: Shekinah (שְׁ כִ ינָ ה)

- **Meaning:** Dwelling, Divine Presence

- **Bible Reference:** Exodus 40:34 – *"Then the cloud covered the Tent of Meeting, and the glory of the Lord filled the tabernacle."*

Message: The **Shekinah** refers to God's visible, manifest presence dwelling among His people. In the Old Testament, His glory appeared as a cloud or fire, showing His closeness to Israel. When the tabernacle was built, God's **Shekinah** filled it, symbolizing His nearness and favor. In the New Testament, Jesus was the fullness of God's presence in human form, and today, the Holy Spirit dwells within believers. God does not just visit His people—He abides with them. The presence of God transforms hearts and brings peace, guidance, and protection. Are you aware of God's presence in your daily life?

Reflection Questions for the Day:

1. When have you felt the **Shekinah** of God in your life?

2. How does knowing that God dwells with you change your perspective?

3. What steps can you take to become more aware of His presence?

Day 107: Panim (פָּ נִ ים)

- **Meaning:** Face, Presence

- **Bible Reference:** Exodus 33:14 – *"My presence (panim) will go with you, and I will give you rest."*

Message: Panim means "face" but also represents God's presence. Moses desired to see God's **panim**, knowing that His presence was more valuable than any blessing. Being in God's **panim** brings peace, clarity, and transformation. Sin separates us from His presence, but through Christ, we have direct access to God. The Holy Spirit allows us to experience His nearness daily, guiding and comforting us. Seeking God's **panim** means pursuing a deep relationship with Him, not just His gifts. Are you seeking His presence or only His blessings?

Reflection Questions for the Day:

1. What does it mean to seek God's **panim**?

2. How do you experience God's presence in your daily life?

3. Are you seeking a relationship with God or just answers to prayers?

Day 108: Makom (מָ,קוֹם)

- **Meaning:** Place, Sacred Space

- **Bible Reference:** Genesis 28:16 – *"Surely the Lord is in this place (makom), and I did not know it."*

Message: Jacob recognized that a seemingly ordinary place was actually filled with God's presence. **Makom** is not just a physical location but anywhere God reveals Himself. The Israelites built altars where they encountered God, making those places sacred. Today, through Jesus, any place can become holy when we acknowledge His presence. Whether in church, at home, or in nature, God meets us in our **makom**. Recognizing His presence transforms ordinary moments into divine encounters. Are you aware that God is with you wherever you go?

Reflection Questions for the Day:

1. Have you ever experienced a moment when a place became sacred to you?

2. How can you create a space in your life to encounter God?

3. Do you recognize God's presence in your daily surroundings?

Day 109: Mishkan (מִ שׁ כָּ ן)

- **Meaning:** Tabernacle, Dwelling Place

- **Bible Reference:** Exodus 25:8 – *"Then have them make a sanctuary for Me, and I will dwell (mishkan) among them."*

Message: The **Mishkan** was the tabernacle where God dwelled among His people during their journey in the wilderness. It was a temporary but sacred place where sacrifices were offered, and God's glory rested. Jesus became the ultimate fulfillment of the **Mishkan**, dwelling among us and making a way for us to approach God. Today, believers are the temple of the Holy Spirit, making our lives a dwelling place for His presence. We must keep our hearts pure, allowing God to fully abide within us. Are you making room for God to dwell in your life?

Reflection Questions for the Day:

1. What does it mean for your body to be a **Mishkan** for God's presence?

117

2. How can you create space for God to dwell in your daily life?

3. What areas of your life need cleansing to be a better dwelling place for God?

Day 110: Qodesh (קֹדֶשׁ)

- **Meaning:** Holiness, Sacredness, Set Apart

- **Bible Reference:** Leviticus 20:26 – *"You are to be holy (qodesh) to Me because I, the Lord, am holy."*

Message: To dwell in God's presence, we must pursue **qodesh**—a life set apart for Him. Holiness is not about religious rituals but about being fully devoted to God. In the Old Testament, the temple and its instruments were considered **qodesh** because they were dedicated to God's purposes. As believers, we are called to live differently from the world, reflecting God's holiness. Jesus' sacrifice makes us holy, but we must also choose to walk in purity and obedience. A life of **qodesh** leads to deeper intimacy with God. Are you living in a way that honors His holiness?

Reflection Questions for the Day:

1. How does holiness impact your relationship with God?

2. Are there any areas in your life that need to be more set apart for God?

3. How can you reflect God's holiness in your daily actions?

Day 111: Yeshivah (יְשִׁיבָה)

- **Meaning:** Dwelling, Abiding, Remaining

- **Bible Reference:** Psalm 91:1 – *"Whoever dwells (yeshivah) in the shelter of the Most High will rest in the shadow of the Almighty."*

Message: Yeshivah means to remain or dwell in a place, not just visit occasionally. Many people seek God only in times of trouble, but He calls us to abide in Him daily. Jesus said, *"Abide in Me, and I will abide in you."* When we make God our dwelling place, we experience His peace, security, and strength. **Yeshivah** is about living in constant awareness of God's presence, rather than drifting in and out of fellowship with Him. A life of abiding leads to lasting transformation and spiritual maturity. Are you dwelling in God's presence or just visiting when convenient?

Reflection Questions for the Day:

1. What does it mean to truly abide in God's presence?

2. How can you develop a consistent relationship with God rather than an occasional one?

3. Are you finding rest in God, or are you restless in your walk with Him?

Day 112: Anan (עָנָן)

- **Meaning:** Cloud, Covering, Divine Guidance

- **Bible Reference:** Exodus 13:21 – *"By day the Lord went ahead of them in a pillar of cloud (anan) to guide them on their way."*

Message: The **Anan** was God's visible presence guiding Israel through the wilderness. It provided shade by day and fire by night, showing that God's presence brings both protection and direction. When the cloud moved, the

Israelites moved; when it rested, they stayed. This teaches us to follow God's leading rather than our own desires. The Holy Spirit is our guide today, leading us through life's uncertainties. Trusting in God's **Anan** means relying on Him even when we don't see the full path ahead. Are you following God's leading or trying to move ahead on your own?

Reflection Questions for the Day:

1. How do you recognize God's guidance in your life?

2. Are you willing to wait when God tells you to stay?

3. What steps can you take to trust His direction more fully?

Week 16 Conclusion

This week's words reveal that God's presence is not distant but near, active, and personal. His **Shekinah** dwells among us, and seeking His **panim** brings peace and transformation. We can encounter Him anywhere, as seen in the concept of **makom**, and our lives become His **Mishkan** when we welcome His Spirit. To remain in His presence, we must pursue **qodesh**, living a life set apart for Him. **Yeshivah** calls us to abide continually, not just occasionally seeking God. His **Anan** guides and protects, leading us step by step. May we live daily in the awareness of His presence, letting His Spirit direct and transform us.

Week 17: God's Protection and Deliverance

Day 113: Magen (מָגֵן)

- **Meaning:** Shield, Protector, Defense

- **Bible Reference:** Psalm 18:30 – *"As for God, His way is perfect; the Lord's word is flawless; He shields (magen) all who take refuge in Him."*

Message: The **magen** is a shield, a symbol of God's divine protection over His people. In battle, a shield defends against attacks, absorbing blows that could otherwise be fatal. God is our **magen**, shielding us from harm, whether physical, spiritual, or emotional. This does not mean we will never face difficulties, but it means He is always our refuge. Abraham was promised that God would be his **magen**, and that promise extends to all who trust in Him. When we put our faith in God, He covers us with His presence. Are you relying on God's protection, or are you trying to fight life's battles on your own?

Reflection Questions for the Day:

1. How have you experienced God's protection in your life?

2. Are there any fears you need to surrender to God's shield?

3. How can you strengthen your faith in God's protective power?

Day 114: Go'el (גּוֹאֵל)

- **Meaning:** Redeemer, Deliverer, Avenger

- **Bible Reference:** Isaiah 41:14 – *"Do not be afraid, you worm Jacob, little Israel, do not fear, for I Myself* *will help you," declares the Lord, your Redeemer (go'el), the Holy One of Israel."*

Message: A **go'el** was a redeemer, often a family member who rescued relatives from slavery or misfortune. Boaz acted as a **go'el** for Ruth, restoring her family's inheritance. God is our ultimate **go'el**, redeeming us from sin and bondage through Jesus Christ. He not only saves but restores what was lost. Redemption means more than salvation—it means freedom and restoration. When we trust in Him, He fights for us, bringing justice and hope. Are you living in the freedom of God's redemption?

Reflection Questions for the Day:

1. What does it mean for Jesus to be your **go'el**?

2. How has God restored you from past struggles?

3. Are you walking in the full freedom of God's redemption?

Day 115: Yeshuah (יְשׁוּעָ,ה)

- **Meaning:** Salvation, Deliverance, Rescue

- **Bible Reference:** Exodus 15:2 – *"The Lord is my strength and my defense; He has become my salvation (yeshuah)."*

Message: Yeshuah means salvation and deliverance, and it appears many times throughout the Old Testament. It is the root of the name Yeshua (Jesus), signifying that He is the ultimate salvation. When Israel was trapped at the Red Sea, God provided **yeshuah**, delivering them from Pharaoh's army. Salvation is not just a one-time event; it is God's ongoing work in our lives. He rescues us from sin, danger, and fear. No matter what challenges we face, His **yeshuah** is always near. Are you trusting in God's deliverance, or are you trying to save yourself?

Reflection Questions for the Day:

1. How does knowing Jesus is your **yeshuah** bring you peace?

2. Are there areas where you need to trust God's deliverance more?

3. How can you share the message of **yeshuah** with others?

Day 116: Machseh (מַ֫חְסֶה)

- **Meaning:** Refuge, Shelter, Safe Place

- **Bible Reference:** Psalm 91:2 – *"I will say of the Lord, 'He is my refuge (machseh) and my fortress, my God, in whom I trust.'"*

Message: A **machseh** is a place of safety, a refuge from storms and danger. The psalmist often referred to God as a **machseh**, knowing that He is the ultimate source of security. In times of trouble, we can run to Him, just as a child runs to a parent for protection. The world offers temporary refuges, but only God provides true, lasting safety. Jesus invites us to find rest in Him, promising peace that the world cannot give. When life feels uncertain, God remains our **machseh**, our safe dwelling place. Are you seeking refuge in God, or in things that cannot truly protect you?

Reflection Questions for the Day:

1. What does it mean for God to be your refuge?

2. How can you trust Him more in times of trouble?

3. What are some ways you can encourage others to seek shelter in God?

Day 117: Netzach (נֶ.צַ.ח)

- **Meaning:** Victory, Eternal Triumph

- **Bible Reference:** 1 Samuel 15:29 – *"He who is the Glory of Israel does not lie or change His mind; for He is not a human being, that He should change His mind."*

Message: Netzach represents eternal victory, a triumph that lasts beyond temporary battles. The Bible shows that God's victories are final—He never loses a battle. David trusted in God's **netzach** when he faced Goliath, knowing the battle belonged to the Lord. Jesus secured the greatest **netzach** by defeating sin and death through His resurrection. As believers, we are not fighting for victory; we are fighting from victory. Even in struggles, we can trust that God's eternal triumph is on our side. Are you living with the confidence that God has already won the victory?

Reflection Questions for the Day:

1. What battles are you trying to fight in your own strength?

2. How does knowing God has already won bring you peace?

3. Are you living with the confidence of victory, or are you still living in fear?

Day 118: Palat (פָ.לַ.ט)

125

- **Meaning:** To Escape, To Deliver, To Bring to Safety

- **Bible Reference:** Psalm 32:7 – *"You are my hiding place; You will protect me from trouble and surround me with songs of deliverance (palat)."*

Message: Palat means to escape or to be rescued from danger. Many times in Scripture, God **palat** His people from harm, leading them to safety. Lot and his family were **palat** from Sodom, and David often cried out for God to **palat** him from his enemies. God's deliverance is not just physical but spiritual—He rescues us from sin and eternal separation from Him. Sometimes, His **palat** is immediate, but other times, it requires patience and trust. No matter what, His rescue is always sure and perfect in timing. Are you trusting God to be your rescuer?

Reflection Questions for the Day:

1. What does it mean to be rescued by God?

2. Have you ever experienced God's **palat** in your life?

3. Are you trusting in His timing for deliverance?

Day 119: Menuchah (מְ,נוּחָ,ה)

- **Meaning:** Rest, Peaceful Security, Tranquility

- **Bible Reference:** Psalm 23:2 – *"He makes me lie down in green pastures, He leads me beside quiet waters (menuchah)."*

Message: Menuchah is the deep, abiding rest that comes from God's protection and provision. The world offers temporary relief, but true rest is only found in Him. In Psalm 23, God leads His people to **menuchah**, a place of peace and safety. Jesus invites all who are weary to come to Him for

126

menuchah, promising rest for their souls. Resting in God does not mean a life without troubles, but a heart at peace in the midst of them. Trusting in God's deliverance allows us to experience **menuchah** fully. Are you finding your rest in Him?

Reflection Questions for the Day:

1. What is preventing you from experiencing **menuchah**?

2. How can trusting God's protection bring true peace?

3. What changes can you make to rest more in God's promises?

Week 17 Conclusion

This week's words remind us that God is our ultimate protector and deliverer. He is our **magen**, shielding us from harm, and our **go'el**, redeeming us from bondage. His **yeshuah** brings salvation, and His **machseh** is a place of refuge in times of trouble. His **netzach** assures us of eternal victory, and through His **palat**, He rescues and delivers us. In His care, we find **menuchah**, a rest that surpasses all earthly peace. May we trust in His unfailing protection, knowing He is always fighting for us.

Week 18: The Power of Obedience and Submission to God

Day 120: Shama (שָׁמַע)

- **Meaning:** To Hear, Listen, Obey

- **Bible Reference:** Deuteronomy 6:4 – *"Hear (shama), O Israel: The Lord our God, the Lord is one."*

Message: Shama means more than just hearing; it means listening with the intent to obey. When God speaks, He expects His people not just to hear His words but to act upon them. The Shema prayer in Deuteronomy emphasizes that true faith involves listening and obeying God wholeheartedly. Jesus echoed this when He said, *"He who has ears, let him hear."* Many people hear God's Word but do not apply it, which leads to spiritual stagnation. True discipleship requires not just knowledge but obedience. Are you truly **shama**—listening to God with a heart ready to obey?

Reflection Questions for the Day:

1. Are you actively listening to God, or just hearing Him?

2. What steps can you take to be more obedient to His voice?

3. How can you cultivate a heart that responds immediately to God's Word?

Day 121: Halakh (הָלַךְ)

- **Meaning:** To Walk, To Live, To Follow

- **Bible Reference:** Micah 6:8 – *"And what does the Lord require of you? To act justly and to love mercy and to walk (halakh) humbly with your God."*

Message: Halakh refers to walking, but in Hebrew thought, it also means a way of life. Walking with God is not just about believing in Him but following His ways daily. Enoch "walked with God," meaning his life was in constant fellowship with the Lord. Jesus called His disciples to follow Him, which required them to change their daily lives. Walking with God means aligning our steps with His guidance, not going our own way. Every decision, every habit, and every word should reflect a life that follows God's path. Are you walking in step with God, or are you going your own direction?

Reflection Questions for the Day:

1. How can you walk more closely with God daily?

2. Are there areas in your life where you are walking away from God's will?

3. What does it mean for your lifestyle to reflect your faith?

Day 122: Yare (יָרֵא)

- **Meaning:** Fear, Reverence, Deep Respect

- **Bible Reference:** Proverbs 9:10 – *"The fear (yare) of the Lord is the beginning of wisdom, and knowledge of the Holy One is understanding."*

Message: Yare does not mean terror but a deep reverence and awe for God. The Bible teaches that the **yare** of the Lord is the foundation of wisdom and obedience. Many people approach God casually, forgetting that He is holy and all-powerful. When we have a true **yare** of God, we take His commands seriously and seek to honor Him in all things. This kind of reverence leads to obedience, purity, and a desire to please Him. Jesus lived in perfect submission to the Father, showing the ultimate example of reverence. Do you have a heart that truly fears and honors God?

Reflection Questions for the Day:

1. How does reverence for God affect your daily decisions?

2. Are there areas in your life where you are not honoring God as you should?

3. How can you develop a deeper awe and respect for God?

Day 123: Avod (עֲבֹד)

- **Meaning:** To Serve, To Work, To Worship

- **Bible Reference:** Joshua 24:15 – *"But as for me and my household, we will serve (avod) the Lord."*

Message: Avod is a powerful word that means both "work" and "worship." In God's design, our service to Him is an act of worship, not just a duty. Joshua declared that his household would **avod** the Lord, meaning their entire lives would be dedicated to serving Him. Jesus came as the ultimate servant, showing that true greatness is found in humbling oneself. Whether in ministry, our jobs, or daily tasks, we can worship God through our service. When we work with a heart of worship, even mundane tasks become meaningful. Are you serving God with joy, seeing it as worship rather than obligation?

Reflection Questions for the Day:

1. How can you turn your daily work into an act of worship?

2. Are you serving God with joy or out of obligation?

3. What areas of your life need to reflect more service to God?

Day 124: Zakar (זָכַ־ר)

- **Meaning:** To Remember, To Recall, To Keep in Mind

- **Bible Reference:** Deuteronomy 8:18 – *"But remember (zakar) the Lord your God, for it is He who gives you the ability to produce wealth."*

Message: Zakar means more than just remembering—it means actively keeping something in mind and living accordingly. God constantly told Israel to **zakar** His commandments and faithfulness, yet they often forgot. Forgetting God's works leads to disobedience, while remembering fuels faith and gratitude. Jesus instituted communion as a way to **zakar** His sacrifice, ensuring that we never forget His love. When we recall God's past faithfulness, it strengthens our trust in Him for the future. Remembering His Word and promises keeps us aligned with His will. Are you actively keeping God's truth in mind, or do you forget His faithfulness in times of trouble?

Reflection Questions for the Day:

1. How can you actively remember God's faithfulness in your life?

2. What are some ways you can remind yourself daily of His Word?

3. Are you living in a way that reflects remembrance of God's goodness?

Day 125: Simchah (שִׂ.מְ.חָ.ה)

- **Meaning:** Joy, Gladness, Rejoicing

- **Bible Reference:** Psalm 100:2 – *"Worship the Lord with gladness; come before Him with joyful (simchah) songs."*

Message: True **simchah** is not based on circumstances but on a heart aligned with God. Biblical joy is a fruit of the Spirit, flowing from obedience and trust in God. The Israelites were commanded to celebrate God's goodness with **simchah**, regardless of their circumstances. Jesus endured the cross "for the joy set before Him," showing that true joy comes from fulfilling God's purpose. The enemy wants to steal our **simchah** through worry, doubt, and sin, but God calls us to rejoice always. When we obey God, joy naturally follows. Are you walking in **simchah**, or are you letting circumstances rob you of joy?

Reflection Questions for the Day:

1. What is the source of your joy?

2. How does obedience to God bring lasting joy?

3. What steps can you take to cultivate more **simchah** in your life?

Day 126: Ratzon (רָ.צוֹן)

- **Meaning:** Will, Desire, Favor

- **Bible Reference:** Psalm 40:8 – *"I desire to do Your will (ratzon), my God; Your law is within my heart."*

Message: **Ratzon** means God's will, His desire for our lives. Jesus perfectly aligned His **ratzon** with the Father's, showing

133

the ultimate act of submission. When we follow God's **ratzon**, we experience His favor and peace. Many struggle with surrendering their own desires to embrace God's higher plans. True fulfillment comes when we let go of personal control and trust His ways. Seeking His **ratzon** requires humility, faith, and a heart devoted to Him. Are you following your own desires, or are you fully surrendered to God's will?

Reflection Questions for the Day:

1. How can you align your desires with God's **ratzon**?

2. Are you resisting God's will in any area of your life?

3. What steps can you take to fully surrender to His plan?

Week 18 Conclusion

This week's words emphasize the importance of hearing, following, and surrendering to God. **Shama** reminds us to listen and obey, while **halakh** calls us to walk in His ways. A heart filled with **yare** reveres God, leading to obedience. **Avod** teaches us that service is an act of worship, and **zakar** urges us to remember His faithfulness. **Simchah** is the joy that follows obedience, and **ratzon** is the ultimate surrender to God's will. May we live lives fully devoted to hearing, following, and obeying God with joy and trust.

Week 19: The Strength Found in God's Promises

Day 127: Tikvah (תִּ. קְ. וָ. ה)

- **Meaning:** Hope, Expectation, Confidence in the Future

- **Bible Reference:** Jeremiah 29:11 – *"For I know the plans I have for you, declares the Lord, plans to prosper you and not to harm you, plans to give you a future and a hope (tikvah)."*

Message: Tikvah is not just wishful thinking but a strong expectation that God's promises will come to pass. In the darkest times, Israel held onto **tikvah**, knowing that God was faithful. Jeremiah spoke these words to a people in exile, reminding them that God's plans were still for their good. Jesus is the fulfillment of our **tikvah**, giving us eternal hope through His sacrifice. When we trust in God's **tikvah**, we do not fear the future but rest in His promises. Hope is the anchor of our soul, keeping us steady in the storms of life. Are you living with the confidence that God's hope never fails?

Reflection Questions for the Day:

1. What is your hope anchored in—circumstances or God's promises?

2. How can you cultivate a mindset of hope in daily life?

3. What promise from God do you need to trust more deeply today?

Day 128: Chazaq (חָ. זַ. ק)

- **Meaning:** Strength, Courage, Firmness

- **Bible Reference:** Joshua 1:9 – *"Have I not commanded you? Be strong (chazaq) and courageous.*

Do not be afraid; do not be discouraged, for the Lord your God will be with you wherever you go. "

Message: Chazaq is the strength that comes from God's presence, not from human ability. When Joshua faced the daunting task of leading Israel, God repeatedly told him to be **chazaq**. True courage is not the absence of fear but the presence of faith. Many times, we feel weak, but God's strength is made perfect in our weakness. Jesus demonstrated ultimate **chazaq**, enduring the cross with unwavering determination. When we rely on God's strength, we can face any challenge without fear. Are you drawing your strength from God, or are you relying on your own abilities?

Reflection Questions for the Day:

1. In what areas do you need to rely on God's strength?

2. How does courage relate to faith?

3. What practical steps can you take to live with **chazaq** each day?

Day 129: Ne'eman (נֶאֱמָן)

- **Meaning:** Faithful, Trustworthy, Reliable

- **Bible Reference:** Deuteronomy 7:9 – *"Know therefore that the Lord your God is God; He is the faithful (ne'eman) God, keeping His covenant of love to a thousand generations of those who love Him and keep His commandments."*

Message: God's **ne'eman** means He is perfectly faithful and trustworthy in every situation. Unlike people, who may fail us, God never breaks His promises. From Abraham to Jesus, God has remained consistent in His faithfulness. Even when

137

we struggle with doubt, His love and promises never change. Recognizing God's faithfulness allows us to trust Him in uncertain times. Jesus is the ultimate example of **ne'eman**, fulfilling every prophecy and promise. Are you trusting in God's faithfulness even when circumstances seem unclear?

Reflection Questions for the Day:

1. How have you seen God's faithfulness in your life?

2. Are there areas where you struggle to trust in His promises?

3. What reminders can you put in place to remember God's faithfulness?

Day 130: Machon (מָכוֹן)

- **Meaning:** Foundation, Established Place, Stability

- **Bible Reference:** Psalm 89:14 – *"Righteousness and justice are the foundation (machon) of Your throne; love and faithfulness go before You."*

Message: A **machon** is a firm foundation, something unshakable and steady. God's throne is built on righteousness and justice, meaning His reign is unmovable. Jesus described a wise man as one who builds his life on the rock, not shifting sand. Many build their lives on temporary things—wealth, relationships, or success—but only God provides true stability. When we root ourselves in Him, we remain steadfast through life's trials. His Word and promises are the ultimate **machon**, keeping us secure. Is your life built on the firm foundation of God's truth?

Reflection Questions for the Day:

1. What is the foundation of your life?

138

2. How can you build your life more securely on God's promises?

3. Are there areas where you have built on unstable ground?

Day 131: Shalom (שָׁלוֹם)

- **Meaning:** Peace, Wholeness, Completeness

- **Bible Reference:** Isaiah 26:3 – *"You will keep in perfect peace (shalom) those whose minds are steadfast, because they trust in You."*

Message: Shalom is more than the absence of conflict; it is a deep sense of well-being and wholeness that comes from God. The world offers temporary peace, but true **shalom** is found in trusting God's promises. Jesus, the Prince of **Shalom**, provides a peace that surpasses understanding. No matter the chaos around us, we can rest in His security. When we trust in God's faithfulness, we experience **shalom** in every circumstance. Our hearts remain steady because we know that He is in control. Are you living in God's peace, or are you allowing fear to steal your **shalom**?

Reflection Questions for the Day:

1. What areas of your life need God's peace?

2. How can you cultivate a deeper sense of **shalom**?

3. What does it mean to trust God even when life feels uncertain?

Day 132: Chesed (חֶסֶד)

- **Meaning:** Lovingkindness, Unfailing Love, Mercy

- **Bible Reference:** Lamentations 3:22 – *"Because of the Lord's great love (chesed) we are not consumed, for His compassions never fail."*

Message: Chesed is God's covenant love, a love that never fails and never gives up. It is a love that is both merciful and faithful, enduring despite human failures. The Bible repeatedly describes God's **chesed**, emphasizing that His love is steadfast. Even when Israel turned away, God's **chesed** remained. Jesus' sacrifice is the ultimate demonstration of **chesed**, showing mercy where judgment was deserved. His love secures us, reminding us that we are never alone. Are you resting in the unfailing love of God, or are you still trying to earn His favor?

Reflection Questions for the Day:

1. How does knowing God's **chesed** give you confidence in your faith?

2. Are you reflecting God's **chesed** in how you treat others?

3. How can you daily remind yourself of God's unfailing love?

Day 133: Emunah (אֱמוּנָ֫ה)

- **Meaning:** Faith, Steadfastness, Trustworthiness

- **Bible Reference:** Habakkuk 2:4 – *"The righteous will live by his faith (emunah)."*

Message: Emunah is not just belief—it is steadfast trust and faithfulness to God. Abraham was counted as righteous because of his **emunah**, trusting God even when he could not see the outcome. True faith remains firm even in trials, holding onto God's promises. Jesus taught that even a small amount of **emunah** can move mountains. Faith grows when we act on what we believe, stepping forward in trust. God's faithfulness inspires our own **emunah**, leading us to greater dependence on Him. Are you standing firm in your faith, or do doubts shake your confidence in God's promises?

Reflection Questions for the Day:

1. How can you strengthen your faith in times of uncertainty?

2. What steps of faith is God calling you to take?

3. How does trusting in God's promises bring stability to your life?

Week 19 Conclusion

This week's words highlight the unshakable foundation found in God's promises. **Tikvah** gives us hope, while **chazaq** strengthens us for life's challenges. **Ne'eman** reminds us that God is always faithful, and **machon** shows that His truth is a firm foundation. **Shalom** brings us peace, **chesed** assures us of His unfailing love, and **emunah** calls us to live by faith. God's promises never fail, giving us confidence no matter what we face. May we walk in His strength, trusting that His Word will always be fulfilled.

Week 20: The Power of God's Guidance

Day 134: Horeh (הוֹרֶה)

- **Meaning:** Teacher, Instructor, Guide

- **Bible Reference:** Psalm 32:8 – *"I will instruct you and teach (horeh) you in the way you should go; I will counsel you with My loving eye on you."*

Message: God is the ultimate **Horeh**, the divine teacher who leads His people in wisdom and truth. Just as a teacher imparts knowledge, God reveals His ways to those who seek Him. Throughout Scripture, He instructs His people through His Word, His Spirit, and even life experiences. Jesus, as the perfect teacher, taught with authority, bringing light to God's truth. The Holy Spirit continues this work, guiding believers into all wisdom. When we allow God to be our instructor, our paths become clear, and our decisions align with His will. Are you positioning yourself to be taught by the Lord daily?

Reflection Questions for the Day:

1. How can you cultivate a heart that is teachable before God?

2. Are you seeking God's instruction in your daily decisions?

3. In what ways has God taught you valuable lessons recently?

Day 135: Derek (דֶּרֶךְ)

- **Meaning:** Path, Way, Journey

- **Bible Reference:** Proverbs 3:6 – *"In all your ways (derek) acknowledge Him, and He will make your paths straight."*

Message: The **derek** represents the path we walk in life—both spiritually and practically. God desires to lead us on the right **derek**, but we must be willing to follow Him. Throughout Scripture, He calls His people to walk in His ways rather than their own. Jesus declared that He is *"the Way"*, showing that true guidance comes through Him. When we trust in God's direction, He makes our paths clear, removing obstacles and providing wisdom. Walking in His **derek** requires faith, obedience, and a willingness to surrender our plans. Are you following God's path or your own?

Reflection Questions for the Day:

1. What areas of your life need to be realigned with God's path?

2. How can you be more intentional about acknowledging Him in your decisions?

3. Are you trusting God even when the path ahead seems unclear?

Day 136: Nahah (נָ,ח,ה)

- **Meaning:** To Lead, To Guide, To Direct

- **Bible Reference:** Psalm 23:3 – *"He guides (nahah) me along the right paths for His name's sake."*

Message: God is our shepherd, and He **nahah**—leads—His people with care and wisdom. A shepherd does not drive the sheep forcefully but gently directs them where they need to go. The Lord's guidance is not just about location but about spiritual growth and maturity. Sometimes, His leading takes us through difficult terrain, but His ways always lead to life. The Holy Spirit is our present-day guide, speaking truth into our hearts. When we surrender to God's leadership, we find peace, knowing He will never misguide us. Are you allowing God to lead you, or are you resisting His direction?

Reflection Questions for the Day:

1. How do you discern God's guidance in your life?

2. Are there areas where you feel hesitant to follow His lead?

3. How can you trust Him more fully as your Shepherd?

Day 137: Or (אוֹר)

- **Meaning:** Light, Illumination, Revelation

- **Bible Reference:** Psalm 119:105 – *"Your word is a lamp to my feet and a light (or) to my path."*

Message: God's **or** brings clarity to the paths we walk, illuminating truth and exposing deception. The world is full of darkness and confusion, but God's Word provides light to guide our steps. Jesus declared, *"I am the Light of the world,"* showing that following Him leads to true understanding. Without light, we stumble; with God's **or**, we see clearly. Many seek guidance from human wisdom, but only God's revelation brings true direction. His light not only leads us but also transforms us, making us reflect His truth to others. Are you walking in God's **or**, or are you relying on your own understanding?

Reflection Questions for the Day:

1. How does God's Word provide light in your decisions?

2. Are there areas in your life where you need more clarity from God?

3. How can you reflect God's light to others?

Day 138: Pa'am (פַּ עַ ם)

- **Meaning:** Steps, Footsteps, Moving Forward
- **Bible Reference:** Psalm 37:23 – *"The steps (pa'am) of a good man are ordered by the Lord, and He delights in his way."*

Message: Each **pa'am**—each step—of a believer's life is directed by God when we seek His guidance. We often want to see the entire journey before taking the first step, but God calls us to walk by faith. Just as He led Israel step by step through the wilderness, He leads us gradually, revealing only what we need for the moment. Our role is not to control the journey but to take faithful steps in obedience. Even when we stumble, He steadies our **pa'am** and directs us back to His will. Trusting in God's timing and leading brings peace. Are you willing to take the next step God is calling you to, even if you don't see the whole picture?

Reflection Questions for the Day:

1. What steps of faith do you need to take right now?

2. How can you trust God when the future is unclear?

3. Are you waiting for perfect conditions before obeying, or are you stepping forward in faith?

Day 139: Bina (בִּ ינָ ה)

- **Meaning:** Understanding, Discernment, Insight

- **Bible Reference:** Proverbs 2:6 – *"For the Lord gives wisdom; from His mouth come knowledge and understanding (bina)."*

Message: Bina is the ability to see beyond the surface and understand the deeper truths of God. Knowledge alone is not enough—without **bina**, we may make poor choices despite having information. God calls us to seek His wisdom, discerning between what is right and wrong, what is temporary and eternal. Solomon asked for **bina**, knowing that ruling with mere human wisdom was insufficient. The Holy Spirit grants discernment to those who seek Him, helping them navigate life's complexities. When we seek God's **bina**, we make decisions that align with His will. Are you relying on your own understanding, or are you asking God for discernment?

Reflection Questions for the Day:

1. How do you seek God's discernment in daily decisions?

2. Are there areas where you need greater understanding from God?

3. How can you grow in spiritual discernment?

Day 140: Boqer (בֹּקֶר)

- **Meaning:** Morning, New Beginning, Dawn

- **Bible Reference:** Lamentations 3:22-23 – *"Because of the Lord's great love we are not consumed, for His compassions never fail. They are new every morning (boqer); great is Your faithfulness."*

Message: Each **boqer**—each new morning—is a gift from God, filled with fresh mercy and new opportunities. No matter how dark the night has been, God's grace meets us with the dawn. In the Bible, mornings symbolize new beginnings, renewed strength, and hope for the future. Jesus often prayed early in the **boqer**, setting an example of seeking God first. A new day is a reminder that we are not defined by yesterday's failures but by God's faithfulness. His mercies are endless, and each sunrise is an invitation to walk in His renewed grace. Are you embracing each **boqer** as a fresh start with God?

Reflection Questions for the Day:

1. How can you make morning time with God a priority?

2. Do you wake up with an attitude of gratitude for God's mercies?

3. What new beginnings is God offering you today?

Week 20 Conclusion

This week's words highlight God's active role in leading His people. As our **Horeh**, He teaches us the right **derek** to follow. He **nahah**—leads us—through His **or**, bringing light to our steps (**pa'am**). With **bina**, He grants wisdom and discernment, helping us navigate life's choices. Each **boqer** reminds us that God's mercies are new, giving us fresh strength to follow His ways. His guidance is constant, loving, and sure. May we trust His leading, knowing that He never fails those who seek Him.

Week 21: The Power of God's Provision

Day 141: Yireh (יָ,ר,אֶ,ה)

- **Meaning:** To See, To Provide

- **Bible Reference:** Genesis 22:14 – *"So Abraham called that place 'The Lord Will Provide (Yireh).' And to this day it is said, 'On the mountain of the Lord it will be provided.'"*

Message: The name **Yireh** comes from Jehovah Jireh, meaning *"The Lord Will Provide."* When Abraham was about to sacrifice Isaac, God saw his faith and provided a ram instead. God's provision is always timely—He sees our needs before we even ask. His provision is not just material but also spiritual, emotional, and relational. Jesus is the ultimate fulfillment of God's **Yireh**, providing salvation through His sacrifice. When we trust Him, we realize that He supplies all we need. Are you relying on God's provision, or are you trying to provide for yourself apart from Him?

Reflection Questions for the Day:

1. How has God provided for you in unexpected ways?

2. Are there areas where you need to trust in His provision more?

3. How can you encourage others to trust in God's **Yireh**?

Day 142: Lechem (לֶ,ח,ם)

- **Meaning:** Bread, Food, Sustenance

- **Bible Reference:** John 6:35 – *"Then Jesus declared, 'I am the bread (lechem) of life. Whoever comes to me will never go hungry, and whoever believes in me will never be thirsty.'"*

Message: Lechem represents physical nourishment, but Jesus used it to symbolize Himself as the spiritual sustenance we need. God provided **lechem**—manna—from heaven for the Israelites, showing that He meets the daily needs of His people. However, Jesus emphasized that man does not live by bread alone, but by every word from God. Our souls hunger for more than just food; we need His truth, grace, and presence. When we seek Jesus, the **Lechem HaChayim** (Bread of Life), we find complete fulfillment. Are you feeding your soul with His Word, or are you trying to satisfy yourself with things that don't last?

Reflection Questions for the Day:

1. What are you relying on for spiritual nourishment?

2. How can you develop a deeper hunger for God's Word?

3. What does it mean for Jesus to be the **Lechem** of your life?

Day 143: Shefa (שֶׁ פַ ע)

- **Meaning:** Abundance, Overflowing Blessing

- **Bible Reference:** Malachi 3:10 – *"Test Me in this,"* *says the Lord Almighty, "and see if I will not throw open the floodgates of heaven and pour out so much blessing (shefa) that there will not be room enough to store it."*

Message: God's **Shefa** is not just about wealth but about the abundant goodness He pours into our lives. He is not a stingy provider; He gives generously beyond what we ask or imagine. Jesus said He came so that we may have life and have it abundantly. This does not mean we will never

151

experience hardship, but it does mean we can live with the peace, joy, and provision of God. When we trust in His abundance, we stop living in fear and start living in faith. His **Shefa** flows into every area of our lives—relationships, wisdom, grace, and opportunities. Are you living with a mindset of scarcity or embracing God's overflowing abundance?

Reflection Questions for the Day:

1. How have you seen God's abundance in your life?

2. Are you trusting God's **Shefa**, or are you living in fear of lack?

3. How can you use God's blessings to bless others?

Day 144: Nachalah (נַ_חֲ_לָ_ה)

- **Meaning:** Inheritance, Possession, Portion
- **Bible Reference:** Psalm 16:5 – *"Lord, You alone are my portion (nachalah) and my cup; You make my lot secure."*

Message: Nachalah refers to an inheritance or portion, something given as a lasting possession. In the Old Testament, the Promised Land was Israel's **nachalah**, a gift from God. But David declared that his true **nachalah** was not land or riches but God Himself. As believers, our inheritance is not just earthly blessings but eternal life through Christ. We are heirs of God's kingdom, receiving His promises as our **nachalah**. Living with this perspective changes how we view success and fulfillment. Are you focusing on temporary gains, or are you embracing your eternal **nachalah**?

Reflection Questions for the Day:

1. What does it mean for God to be your portion?

2. How does knowing your eternal inheritance change your perspective?

3. Are you living with an earthly or eternal mindset?

Day 145: Tzedakah (צְ ,דָ ,קָ ,ה)

- **Meaning:** Righteousness, Generosity, Charity

- **Bible Reference:** Proverbs 11:25 – *"A generous person will prosper; whoever refreshes others will be refreshed."*

Message: Tzedakah means righteousness but is also used to describe acts of generosity and charity. Biblical giving is not just an obligation but an act of faith and worship. God provides for us so that we can be a blessing to others. Jesus praised the widow who gave all she had, showing that generosity is measured by the heart, not the amount. When we live generously, we reflect God's character and trust in His provision. True **tzedakah** is not just about money but about serving, encouraging, and meeting the needs of others. Are you practicing **tzedakah**, using what God has given you to bless others?

Reflection Questions for the Day:

1. How does generosity reflect God's character?

2. Are you giving out of obligation or with a joyful heart?

3. How can you practice **tzedakah** in your daily life?

Day 146: Mazon (מָ ,זֹון)

- **Meaning:** Nourishment, Provision, Sustenance

153

- **Bible Reference:** Psalm 136:25 – *"He gives food (mazon) to every creature. His love endures forever."*

Message: God provides **mazon**—not just physical food but everything needed to sustain life. Every meal, every breath, and every blessing is a reminder of His care. The Israelites depended on God's daily **mazon** in the form of manna, teaching them to trust Him daily. Jesus taught us to pray, *"Give us this day our daily bread,"* reminding us that God is our ultimate provider. In a world that seeks security in wealth, we are called to trust in God's daily provision. He gives us what we need, when we need it. Are you trusting in God's **mazon**, or are you trying to secure everything on your own?

Reflection Questions for the Day:

1. How does relying on God's provision bring peace?

2. Are you grateful for the daily **mazon** God provides?

3. How can you be a source of nourishment and provision for others?

Day 147: Shalvah (שַׁ_לְ_וָ_ה)

- **Meaning:** Tranquility, Security, Prosperity

- **Bible Reference:** Psalm 122:7 – *"May there be peace (shalvah) within your walls and security within your citadels."*

Message: True **shalvah** is not just material prosperity but deep security in God's provision. Many chase after wealth, thinking it will bring peace, but only God provides lasting security. The Bible teaches that trusting in riches is unstable, but relying on God brings **shalvah**. Paul said he had learned to be content in all circumstances because his peace came from God. Jesus offers peace that the world cannot give, a security that goes beyond possessions. When we live in God's **shalvah**, we experience true prosperity—peace, stability, and confidence in His care. Are you seeking temporary security or eternal peace in God?

Reflection Questions for the Day:

1. What does true prosperity mean to you?

2. Are you trusting in material security or in God's peace?

3. How can you rest in God's **shalvah** today?

Week 21 Conclusion

This week's words reveal the many ways God provides for His people. **Yireh** reminds us that God sees our needs and provides at the right time. **Lechem** and **mazon** show that He nourishes us physically and spiritually. His **shefa** overflows, and our **nachalah** is an eternal inheritance. **Tzedakah** teaches us to give generously, while **shalvah** assures us of lasting peace in His care. May we trust in His faithful provision and live with hearts full of gratitude and generosity.

Week 22: The Power of Trusting in God

Day 148: Batach (בָּטַ_ח)

- **Meaning:** To Trust, To Have Confidence

- **Bible Reference:** Proverbs 3:5 – *"Trust (batach) in the Lord with all your heart and lean not on your own understanding."*

Message: Batach is more than just belief—it is full confidence in God's character and promises. Many people say they trust God but still rely on their own strength and understanding. The Bible teaches that true trust means surrendering control, knowing that God's plans are better than ours. Abraham demonstrated **batach** when he left his homeland without knowing where God would lead him. Jesus calls us to trust Him fully, even when the path is unclear. Trusting in God brings peace, knowing He is working for our good. Are you truly **batach** in the Lord, or are you holding onto control?

Reflection Questions for the Day:

1. What areas of your life are hardest to surrender to God?

2. How can you grow in trusting God completely?

3. What does it mean to lean on God instead of your own understanding?

Day 149: Emun (אֱמוּן)

- **Meaning:** Faithfulness, Steadfastness, Stability

- **Bible Reference:** Deuteronomy 32:4 – *"He is the Rock, His works are perfect, and all His ways are just. A faithful (emun) God who does no wrong, upright and just is He."*

Message: Emun describes God's unwavering faithfulness. Unlike human promises, which can be broken, God's faithfulness is eternal and unshakable. He is a firm foundation, always true to His Word. Throughout history, God has proven His **emun**, fulfilling every promise He has made. Jesus embodies this faithfulness, showing that God's love and truth never fail. When we trust in His **emun**, we gain confidence that He will never abandon us. Are you standing firm in God's faithfulness, or are you doubting His promises?

Reflection Questions for the Day:

1. How has God shown His faithfulness in your life?

2. Do you trust in God's faithfulness even in difficult seasons?

3. How can you reflect God's **emun** in your relationships with others?

Day 150: Galal (גָּלַל)

- **Meaning:** To Commit, To Roll Onto, To Entrust

- **Bible Reference:** Psalm 37:5 – *"Commit (galal) your way to the Lord; trust in Him, and He will do this."*

Message: Galal means to roll something onto God, symbolizing full surrender. The Bible calls us to cast our burdens on the Lord because He cares for us. Many times, we try to carry worries and struggles on our own, but God invites us to **galal** them onto Him. David committed his way to God, trusting that He would bring justice and direction. Jesus also taught about entrusting our lives fully to God, living with faith instead of anxiety. When we **galal**, we let go and trust in

158

God's perfect plan. Are you truly committing your worries, plans, and future into God's hands?

Reflection Questions for the Day:

1. What burdens do you need to roll onto God today?

2. Why is it sometimes difficult to commit things fully to God?

3. How can you remind yourself daily to trust God with everything?

Day 151: Machsi (מ_ח,ס,י)

- **Meaning:** Refuge, Shelter, Safe Haven

- **Bible Reference:** Psalm 91:2 – *"I will say of the Lord, 'He is my refuge (machsi) and my fortress, my God, in whom I trust.'"*

Message: Machsi describes God as our ultimate place of safety. The world offers temporary security, but only God provides true refuge. The psalmist often wrote about God being a **machsi** in times of trouble. No matter what storms come, we can find peace in His presence. Jesus told His followers not to be afraid, reminding them that God watches over them. When we take refuge in Him, fear loses its power over us. Are you running to God as your **machsi**, or are you seeking security elsewhere?

Reflection Questions for the Day:

1. What does it mean to take refuge in God?

2. How can you make God your first source of security?

3. Are you allowing fear to control you, or are you resting in God's protection?

Day 152: Qavah (ק,ו,ה)

- **Meaning:** To Wait, To Hope, To Expect

- **Bible Reference:** Isaiah 40:31 – *"But those who wait (qavah) on the Lord will renew their strength; they will soar on wings like eagles."*

Message: Qavah is more than just waiting—it is hopeful expectation that God will act. Many people become discouraged when prayers are not answered immediately. However, Scripture teaches that God's timing is perfect, and those who **qavah** in Him will be renewed. Waiting is not passive; it involves trust, worship, and faith in His promises. Jesus told His disciples to wait for the Holy Spirit, showing that patience leads to great blessings. When we learn to **qavah**, we experience deeper reliance on God. Are you waiting with expectation, or are you losing hope?

Reflection Questions for the Day:

1. What is something you are currently waiting on God for?

2. How can you maintain hope and faith while waiting?

3. How has waiting on God strengthened your faith in the past?

Day 153: Seter (ס,ת,ר)

- **Meaning:** Secret Place, Hidden Shelter

- **Bible Reference:** Psalm 91:1 – *"Whoever dwells in the secret place (seter) of the Most High will rest in the shadow of the Almighty."*

Message: The **seter** of God is a place of intimacy, where He shelters and protects His people. It is not just a physical refuge but a spiritual place of closeness with Him. The Bible speaks of seeking God in the quiet, hidden places, away from distractions. Jesus often withdrew to spend time with the Father, demonstrating the importance of abiding in His presence. The more time we spend in God's **seter**, the more we grow in faith and trust. In His presence, we find peace, guidance, and renewal. Are you taking time to dwell in God's **seter**, or are you too distracted?

Reflection Questions for the Day:

1. What does the secret place with God look like in your life?

2. How can you develop a deeper intimacy with God?

3. Are you prioritizing time in God's presence, or is busyness keeping you away?

Day 154: Tikon (תָּכוּן)

- **Meaning:** To Establish, Make Firm, Prepare

- **Bible Reference:** Psalm 40:2 – *"He lifted me out of the slimy pit, out of the mud and mire; He set my feet on a rock and gave me a firm (tikon) place to stand."*

Message: **Tikon** means to establish or make something firm and unshakable. When God leads us, He does not place us on unstable ground. Instead, He sets us on a **tikon**, a strong foundation in Him. Life's challenges can make us feel like we are sinking, but God provides stability. Jesus spoke of building a house on the rock rather than sand, emphasizing the importance of standing on God's truth. When we trust in Him, He prepares us for every challenge. Are you standing on

161

the firm foundation of God's promises, or are you on shaky ground?

Reflection Questions for the Day:

1. What is the foundation of your life?

2. How can you strengthen your faith so that it remains unshaken?

3. Are you allowing God to establish and prepare you for His plans?

Week 22 Conclusion

This week's words emphasize the importance of fully relying on God. **Batach** calls us to trust Him completely, while **emun** reminds us of His unwavering faithfulness. **Galal** teaches us to commit our ways to Him, and **machsi** assures us of His shelter and security. **Qavah** encourages us to wait on Him with hope, while **seter** reveals the intimate protection found in His presence. Finally, **tikon** reminds us that God establishes us on a firm foundation. Trusting God brings peace, stability, and confidence in His perfect plan. May we continually rest in His promises, knowing He is always faithful.

Week 23: The Power of God's Forgiveness and Mercy

Day 155: Selichah (ס. ל. יח. ה)

- **Meaning:** Forgiveness, Pardon, Acknowledgment of Sin

- **Bible Reference:** Psalm 130:4 – *"But with You there is forgiveness (selichah), so that we can, with reverence, serve You."*

Message: Selichah means not only forgiveness but also an act of mercy in response to repentance. God is abundant in **selichah**, offering full pardon to those who genuinely turn back to Him. The psalmist recognized that without God's **selichah**, no one could stand before Him. In the New Testament, Jesus emphasized forgiveness as a central theme, teaching that as we receive **selichah**, we must also extend it to others. True forgiveness brings freedom, healing, and restoration. Holding onto unforgiveness keeps us bound, while releasing others through **selichah** allows God's love to flow freely in our hearts. Are you embracing God's **selichah** in your life and extending it to others?

Reflection Questions for the Day:

1. Have you fully received God's forgiveness, or are you still carrying guilt?

2. Are there people in your life you need to forgive?

3. How does extending forgiveness reflect God's grace?

Day 156: Rachamim (ר. ח. מ. ים)

- **Meaning:** Mercy, Compassion, Deep Love

- **Bible Reference:** Lamentations 3:22 – *"Because of the Lord's great mercy (rachamim) we are not consumed, for His compassions never fail."*

Message: Rachamim comes from the root word for "womb," symbolizing a deep, nurturing love. God's mercy is not given begrudgingly but flows from His heart of compassion. Even when Israel rebelled, God's **rachamim** remained, always calling them back. Jesus demonstrated this mercy countless times—healing the sick, forgiving sinners, and showing love to those society rejected. We, too, are called to live in **rachamim**, showing kindness even when others don't deserve it. His mercy renews every morning, reminding us that we are never beyond His grace. Are you living with a heart of mercy toward others?

Reflection Questions for the Day:

1. How have you experienced God's **rachamim** in your life?

2. Are you quick to show mercy, or do you struggle with judgment?

3. How can you actively demonstrate God's compassion to those around you?

Day 157: Kaphar (כָּ.פָ.ר)

- **Meaning:** Atonement, Covering, Reconciliation

- **Bible Reference:** Leviticus 17:11 – *"For the life of a creature is in the blood, and I have given it to you to make atonement (kaphar) for yourselves on the altar."*

Message: Kaphar means to cover or make atonement for sin. In the Old Testament, sacrifices were offered as a **kaphar**, temporarily covering the sins of the people. Jesus became the ultimate **kaphar**, shedding His blood to fully and permanently remove sin. Because of His atonement, we are reconciled with God, no longer separated by guilt. This gift of grace is freely given, not earned. When we accept Christ's **kaphar**, we walk in the freedom of complete forgiveness. Are you living in the reality of Christ's atonement, or are you still carrying the weight of past sins?

Reflection Questions for the Day:

1. How does knowing Jesus is your **kaphar** change your perspective on forgiveness?

2. Are you still holding onto guilt for sins that God has already covered?

3. How can you walk in the freedom of Christ's atonement every day?

Day 158: Chanan (חָנַן)

- **Meaning:** Grace, Favor, Undeserved Kindness

- **Bible Reference:** Numbers 6:25 – *"The Lord make His face shine on you and be gracious (chanan) to you."*

Message: Chanan represents God's undeserved favor, freely given to those who trust Him. Grace is at the heart of the Gospel—Jesus' death and resurrection are the ultimate expressions of **chanan**. We cannot earn His love, nor can we work for His favor; it is a gift. Many struggle to accept grace, feeling unworthy, but God delights in pouring out His kindness. Just as He extends **chanan** to us, we are called to be gracious to others. When we live in grace, we experience the depth of God's love. Are you receiving and sharing God's **chanan** freely?

Reflection Questions for the Day:

1. How does God's **chanan** impact the way you live?

2. Are you trying to earn God's favor, or do you rest in His grace?

3. How can you extend grace to others in your daily life?

Day 159: Tahor (טָהוֹר)

- **Meaning:** Pure, Clean, Holy

- **Bible Reference:** Psalm 51:10 – *"Create in me a pure (tahor) heart, O God, and renew a steadfast spirit within me."*

Message: Tahor represents purity of heart, mind, and soul before God. In the Old Testament, ceremonial purity was essential for worship, but Jesus emphasized inner purity. A **tahor** heart is not perfect but is devoted and open to God's refining work. When we confess our sins, God cleanses us, making us **tahor** again. Purity allows us to see God clearly, removing distractions that hinder our relationship with Him. Walking in holiness is a daily commitment, relying on His Spirit for transformation. Are you striving for a **tahor** heart in all areas of life?

Reflection Questions for the Day:

1. What does spiritual purity mean to you?

2. Are there things in your life that are clouding your relationship with God?

3. How can you maintain a **tahor** heart in a sinful world?

Day 160: Chayah (חָיָה)

- **Meaning:** To Live, To Revive, To Restore

- **Bible Reference:** Ezekiel 37:5 – *"This is what the Sovereign Lord says to these bones: I will make breath enter you, and you will come to life (chayah)."*

Message: Chayah represents not just physical life but spiritual revival and renewal. When Ezekiel saw the valley of dry bones, God's breath brought them to life, symbolizing restoration. In Christ, we move from spiritual death to **chayah**, experiencing true life. Jesus came so that we may have abundant life, full of His presence. Many walk through life feeling spiritually dry, but God desires to refresh and restore. His Spirit breathes new life into weary souls. Are you allowing God to bring **chayah** into the dry areas of your life?

Reflection Questions for the Day:

1. What areas of your life need revival?

2. How can you experience the full life that Jesus offers?

3. Are you relying on your own strength, or are you allowing God to restore you?

Day 161: Mechilah (מְ חִ ילָ ה)

- **Meaning:** Full Pardon, Complete Forgiveness

- **Bible Reference:** Isaiah 43:25 – *"I, even I, am He who blots out your transgressions, for My own sake, and remembers your sins no more."*

Message: Mechilah is more than just forgiveness—it is a complete and permanent pardon. God does not just forgive; He chooses to forget our sins. Many struggle with past failures, but God's **mechilah** means we are fully cleansed. Jesus' sacrifice secured this eternal forgiveness, making us righteous before God. When we accept His **mechilah**, we can walk in freedom, no longer bound by guilt. We are also called to extend this same forgiveness to others. Are you fully embracing the **mechilah** God offers, or are you holding onto past shame?

Reflection Questions for the Day:

1. Do you truly believe that God has completely forgiven you?

2. Are you extending **mechilah** to others, or are you holding onto resentment?

3. How can you walk daily in the freedom of God's full pardon?

Week 23 Conclusion

This week's words emphasize the depth of God's love and the freedom found in His mercy. **Selichah** teaches us the power of forgiveness, while **rachamim** reminds us of His deep compassion. **Kaphar** highlights Christ's atonement, and **chanan** shows His grace. **Tahor** calls us to purity, while **chayah** speaks of spiritual revival. Finally, **mechilah** reassures us of complete and lasting forgiveness. When we embrace God's mercy, we walk in true freedom. May we not only receive His grace but also extend it to others.

Week 24: The Power of Worship and Praise

Day 162: Halal (ל‗ל‗ה)

- **Meaning:** To Praise, To Shine, To Boast in God

- **Bible Reference:** Psalm 150:6 – *"Let everything that has breath praise (halal) the Lord. Praise the Lord!"*

Message: The Hebrew word **halal** is the root of *hallelujah* and means to praise with great joy and enthusiasm. This type of praise is not quiet or reserved; it is a bold declaration of God's greatness. In the Psalms, David used **halal** repeatedly, encouraging all creation to worship God with gladness. When we choose to **halal** the Lord, we shift our focus from our problems to His power. True praise is not dependent on circumstances—it flows from a heart that trusts in God's sovereignty. Even in difficult times, praise opens the door for breakthrough. Are you living a life of **halal**, boasting in the Lord's goodness?

Reflection Questions for the Day:

1. What does it mean to praise God with enthusiasm?

2. How can you practice joyful praise even in challenging times?

3. What are some ways you can make **halal** a daily habit?

Day 163: Tehillah (ה‗ל‗ה‗ת)

- **Meaning:** Song of Praise, Worshipful Adoration

- **Bible Reference:** Psalm 22:3 – *"Yet You are enthroned as the Holy One; You are the one Israel praises (tehillah)."*

Message: Tehillah is a form of praise that involves singing and worship. It is not just about words but a heart overflowing with love for God. The Psalms are full of **tehillah**, expressing gratitude, devotion, and reverence. God inhabits the **tehillah** of His people, meaning that when we worship, we invite His presence into our lives. Worship brings us into alignment with God's will and strengthens our faith. When we sing praises, we declare His power over our circumstances. Are you filling your life with **tehillah**, making worship a part of your daily walk?

Reflection Questions for the Day:

1. How does singing praise deepen your connection with God?

2. What is a song of worship that has impacted your faith?

3. How can you make **tehillah** a regular part of your spiritual life?

Day 164: Yadah (יָדָ֥ה)

- **Meaning:** To Extend the Hands in Praise, Thanksgiving

- **Bible Reference:** Psalm 138:1 – *"I will praise (yadah) You, Lord, with all my heart; before the 'gods' I will sing Your praise."*

Message: Yadah means to extend one's hands in praise and surrender to God. This physical act is a sign of worship, acknowledging that all blessings come from Him. Raising hands in prayer and praise is seen throughout Scripture, symbolizing thanksgiving, surrender, and dependence. When we lift our hands, we declare that we trust God fully and submit to His authority. **Yadah** is also an act of gratitude, thanking God for His goodness. Worship is not just about the heart but also about expressing devotion through our actions. Are you willing to lift your hands in surrender and praise, giving God all the glory?

Reflection Questions for the Day:

1. What does lifting your hands in worship mean to you?

2. How can physical expressions of praise deepen your worship experience?

3. What are some ways you can practice **yadah** in your daily life?

Day 165: Barak (ְבָּרַךְ)

- **Meaning:** To Kneel, To Bless, To Honor God

- **Bible Reference:** Psalm 95:6 – *"Come, let us bow down in worship, let us kneel (barak) before the Lord our Maker."*

Message: Barak means to kneel before God in reverence and submission. Worship is not just about singing—it is about humbling ourselves before the King of Kings. When we kneel, we acknowledge that God is sovereign and worthy of all honor. The act of bowing symbolizes surrender, devotion, and a willingness to follow His ways. Jesus humbled Himself before the Father, showing the ultimate example of reverence. In worship, we **barak** the Lord, blessing His name with our lives. Are you bowing before God in reverence, surrendering completely to His will?

Reflection Questions for the Day:

1. How does kneeling in prayer or worship reflect humility before God?

2. What areas of your life do you need to surrender in worship?

3. How can you live in a way that blesses and honors God?

Day 166: Zamar (זָמַר)

- **Meaning:** To Sing and Play Music in Praise

- **Bible Reference:** Psalm 98:4 – *"Shout for joy to the Lord, all the earth, burst into jubilant song with music (zamar)."*

Message: Zamar is the act of making music in praise to God. Worship is not just about singing—it involves instruments, melodies, and joyful celebration. The Bible encourages us to worship with songs, harps, cymbals, and every instrument available. Music has a unique way of expressing emotions and drawing us closer to God. King David, a musician and songwriter, filled the Psalms with **zamar**, using music as a powerful tool for worship. Whether through singing or playing an instrument, our praise should be heartfelt and joyful. Are you using music as a way to glorify God in your life?

Reflection Questions for the Day:

1. How does music help you connect with God in worship?

2. Are you using your musical gifts to glorify Him?

3. How can you incorporate more **zamar** into your spiritual life?

174

Day 167: Todah (תּוֹדָה)

- **Meaning:** Thanksgiving, Confession, Praise in Advance

- **Bible Reference:** Psalm 50:23 – *"Those who sacrifice thank offerings (todah) honor Me, and to the blameless I will show My salvation."*

Message: Todah is the act of giving thanks to God, even before seeing the answer to prayer. It is an offering of faith, trusting that God will fulfill His promises. Many times, praise is given after a breakthrough, but **todah** is praise given in expectation. When Jehoshaphat led Israel into battle, they sang praises before the victory was won, and God delivered them. This kind of worship demonstrates deep trust in God's faithfulness. True faith thanks God not only for what He has done but also for what He will do. Are you willing to praise God before you see the answer?

Reflection Questions for the Day:

1. How can you practice **todah** in your daily life?

2. What promises of God are you trusting in, even before they happen?

3. Why is it important to give thanks in advance of answered prayers?

Day 168: Shabach (שָׁבַח)

- **Meaning:** To Shout in Victory and Praise

- **Bible Reference:** Psalm 47:1 – *"Clap your hands, all you nations; shout (shabach) to God with cries of joy."*

Message: Shabach means to loudly proclaim God's greatness in victory and celebration. Worship is not always quiet—sometimes, it is a triumphant shout of joy and declaration of faith. The Israelites shouted **shabach** around Jericho before the walls fell, demonstrating faith before the victory was seen. Jesus entered Jerusalem with people shouting *"Hosanna!"*, proclaiming Him as King. There is power in vocalizing praise, breaking spiritual barriers and inviting God's presence. Worship should be fearless and uninhibited, declaring His glory boldly. Are you willing to **shabach**, proclaiming God's goodness with joy and confidence?

Reflection Questions for the Day:

1. Why do you think shouting in worship can be powerful?

2. Are you willing to boldly declare God's greatness?

3. How can you practice **shabach** in your daily worship?

Week 24 Conclusion

This week's words reveal the richness of biblical worship. **Halal** teaches us to praise with joy, while **tehillah** calls us to sing in adoration. **Yadah** and **barak** show us how physical expressions—lifting hands and kneeling—demonstrate surrender and reverence. **Zamar** reminds us of the power of music in worship, and **todah** teaches us to praise in faith before the breakthrough. **Shabach** encourages us to proclaim God's greatness with boldness. Worship is a powerful way to connect with God, align our hearts with His, and experience His presence. May we worship Him in spirit and truth every day!

Week 25: The Power of God's Calling and Purpose

Day 169: Qara (ק, ר, א)

- **Meaning:** To Call, To Summon, To Proclaim

- **Bible Reference:** Isaiah 43:1 – *"Do not fear, for I have redeemed you; I have called (qara) you by name; you are Mine."*

Message: God does not just call people in a general sense— He calls each of us by name. **Qara** means more than just speaking; it is a personal invitation to follow Him. From Abraham to Moses, from the prophets to the disciples, God's **qara** has shaped the course of history. Jesus called His followers to leave everything behind and walk in His purpose. When God **qara** us, He equips and strengthens us for His work. Our response to His calling determines whether we will step into His plans or resist His direction. Are you listening to and responding to God's **qara** in your life?

Reflection Questions for the Day:

1. How has God called you personally?

2. Are you actively responding to His call, or are you hesitating?

3. What steps can you take to walk fully in God's calling?

Day 170: Avodah (ע, ב, וֹ, ד, ה)

- **Meaning:** Work, Service, Worship

- **Bible Reference:** Exodus 23:25 – *"Worship (avodah) the Lord your God, and His blessing will be on your food and water."*

Message: Avodah is a unique Hebrew word that means work, service, and worship all at once. In God's design, our work is an act of worship when done with the right heart. The Bible teaches that everything we do—whether in ministry, business, or daily responsibilities—should be done as **avodah** to the Lord. Jesus modeled a life of **avodah**, serving others and glorifying the Father. When we view our labor as worship, we find purpose and fulfillment in even the simplest tasks. The way we work reflects our devotion to God. Are you treating your work as **avodah**, a form of worship to Him?

Reflection Questions for the Day:

1. How can you view your daily work as an act of worship?

2. Are you serving God with joy, or does your work feel disconnected from your faith?

3. How can you dedicate your skills and tasks to glorify God?

Day 171: Nasa (נָשָׂא)

- **Meaning:** To Lift Up, To Carry, To Bear

- **Bible Reference:** Psalm 121:1 – *"I lift up (nasa) my eyes to the mountains—where does my help come from?"*

Message: Nasa signifies lifting something up or carrying a burden. Jesus carried the burden of our sins, lifting them from us and giving us freedom. In response, we are called to lift up His name in worship and to help carry the burdens of others. The Bible tells us to bear one another's burdens, showing Christ's love through action. Sometimes, God calls us to **nasa** dreams and responsibilities that seem overwhelming, but He provides the strength. When we fix our eyes on Him, He lifts us above fear and doubt. Are you allowing God to carry your burdens, or are you holding onto them yourself?

Reflection Questions for the Day:

1. What burdens do you need to surrender to God?

2. How can you help carry the burdens of others in love?

3. Are you lifting up the name of Jesus in your daily life?

Day 172: Shalach (שָׁלַח)

- **Meaning:** To Send, To Release, To Commission

- **Bible Reference:** Isaiah 6:8 – *"Then I heard the voice of the Lord saying, 'Whom shall I send (shalach)?' And I said, 'Here am I. Send me!'"*

Message: Shalach is God's act of sending people out for His purposes. Throughout Scripture, God sent prophets, judges, and leaders to accomplish His plans. Jesus was sent into the world to bring salvation, and He, in turn, sent His disciples to make His name known. When God calls, He also sends. Every believer is called to be **shalach**, sent out to be a light in the world. Sometimes, **shalach** means stepping into a new season, trusting that God's purpose is greater than our fears. Are you willing to be **shalach**, letting God send you where He desires?

Reflection Questions for the Day:

1. What is God calling you to step into?

2. Are you open to being sent by God, even into the unknown?

3. How can you be a representative of Christ wherever you go?

Day 173: Peulah (פְּעוּלָה)

- **Meaning:** Deed, Action, Accomplishment

- **Bible Reference:** Psalm 90:17 – *"May the favor of the Lord our God rest on us; establish the work (peulah) of our hands for us—yes, establish the work of our hands."*

Message: Peulah emphasizes that our faith should not remain theoretical—it must be lived out in action. The Bible teaches that faith without works is dead; our love for God is shown in what we do. Jesus did not just preach about love— He lived it through healing, serving, and sacrificing. Every deed we do in His name has eternal significance. The smallest acts of kindness, obedience, and faithfulness become part of God's greater purpose. When we allow God to establish our **peulah**, our lives bear lasting fruit. Are your actions reflecting your faith?

Reflection Questions for the Day:

1. What actions can you take to actively live out your faith?

2. How does your daily work contribute to God's kingdom?

3. Are you seeking God's direction in the work of your hands?

Day 174: Qavah (קָוָה)

- **Meaning:** To Wait, To Hope, To Trust

- **Bible Reference:** Isaiah 40:31 – *"But those who hope (qavah) in the Lord will renew their strength."*

Message: Qavah is not passive waiting but expectant hope in God's timing and promises. Often, we grow impatient when God's plans do not unfold as quickly as we desire. Yet, Scripture tells us that waiting on the Lord brings renewal and strength. God's timing is always perfect, even when we do not understand it. Waiting allows us to grow in faith, depend on Him, and prepare for what He has ahead. Just as a farmer waits for the harvest, we must **qavah** with trust, knowing God is at work. Are you waiting on God with expectation, or are you struggling with impatience?

Reflection Questions for the Day:

1. What promises of God are you waiting on?

2. How can waiting on God strengthen your faith?

3. Are you trusting in God's timing or trying to rush His plans?

Day 175: Nachash (נ‚ח‚שׁ)

- **Meaning:** To Perceive, To Discern, To Seek Understanding

- **Bible Reference:** Proverbs 3:5-6 – *"Trust in the Lord with all your heart and lean not on your own understanding (nachash); in all your ways submit to Him, and He will make your paths straight."*

Message: Nachash speaks of the need for discernment in following God's calling. Many times, we make decisions based on emotions or human wisdom rather than seeking God's guidance. The Bible warns us not to lean on our own

nachash, but to trust in God's wisdom. Spiritual discernment helps us recognize His voice, avoid deception, and walk in the right path. Jesus operated in perfect discernment, always aligning with the Father's will. When we seek God's **nachash**, we receive clarity, direction, and peace. Are you seeking God's wisdom in your decisions, or are you relying on your own understanding?

Reflection Questions for the Day:

1. How do you discern God's voice in your life?

2. Are you making decisions based on God's wisdom or your own understanding?

3. What steps can you take to grow in spiritual discernment?

Week 25 Conclusion

This week's words remind us that God calls each of us for a purpose. **Qara** emphasizes His calling, while **avodah** shows that even our work is worship. **Nasa** teaches us to lift our burdens and serve others, and **shalach** reminds us that God sends us out for His mission. **Peulah** calls us to live out our faith in action, while **qavah** strengthens us to wait on His perfect timing. Lastly, **nachash** urges us to seek His wisdom in every decision. May we walk confidently in God's purpose, knowing that He leads us every step of the way!

Week 26: The Power of God's Peace and Rest

Day 176: Menuchah (מְנוּחָה)

- **Meaning:** Rest, Tranquility, Quietness
- **Bible Reference:** Psalm 23:2 – *"He makes me lie down in green pastures, He leads me beside quiet waters (menuchah)."*

Message: Menuchah represents the deep, abiding rest that God offers His people. It is not just physical rest but spiritual renewal and peace that comes from trusting in Him. When God led the Israelites out of Egypt, He promised them a land of **menuchah**, a place where they could dwell in safety and prosperity. Jesus extended this invitation, saying, *"Come to Me, all who are weary, and I will give you rest."* In a world filled with stress and constant demands, God calls us to enter His **menuchah**, resting in His presence and promises. True rest is found not in idleness but in trusting God completely. Are you allowing yourself to experience God's **menuchah**, or are you striving in your own strength?

Reflection Questions for the Day:

1. What does true rest in God look like in your life?

2. How can you intentionally enter into God's **menuchah** each day?

3. Are you relying on your own strength instead of resting in God's provision?

Day 177: Shalom (שָׁלוֹם)

- **Meaning:** Peace, Wholeness, Well-being
- **Bible Reference:** Isaiah 26:3 – *"You will keep in perfect peace (shalom) those whose minds are steadfast, because they trust in You."*

Message: Shalom is not just the absence of conflict but a state of complete well-being and harmony with God. The world offers temporary peace, but only God provides perfect **shalom** that transcends circumstances. Jesus, the Prince of **Shalom**, came to bring reconciliation between God and man, giving us lasting peace. When our minds are fixed on God, we experience His **shalom**, even in the midst of chaos. Worry and anxiety steal our peace, but faith in God's promises restores it. Living in **shalom** means trusting that God is in control. Are you walking in God's **shalom**, or are you letting fear disrupt your peace?

Reflection Questions for the Day:

1. What are the biggest sources of anxiety in your life?

2. How can you trust God more deeply to experience His **shalom**?

3. What steps can you take to share God's peace with others?

Day 178: Noach (נֹחַ)

- **Meaning:** Rest, Comfort, Relief

- **Bible Reference:** Genesis 5:29 – *"He will comfort us in the labor and painful toil of our hands caused by the ground the Lord has cursed."*

Message: The name **Noach** (Noah) means rest, signifying relief from the burdens of life. In a world filled with striving, God desires that we find true rest in Him. Just as Noah found favor in God's eyes, those who trust Him experience peace amidst the storms. The flood was a time of great turmoil, yet Noah and his family rested in the ark, safe in God's protection. In Christ, we are given the same invitation to enter

186

His ark of salvation and rest from striving. God's desire is for His children to walk in **Noach**, not in constant exhaustion. Are you allowing God to give you **Noach**, or are you carrying burdens you were never meant to bear?

Reflection Questions for the Day:

1. In what areas of life are you feeling weary?

2. How can you trust God to bring comfort and relief?

3. What does it mean to enter God's ark of rest and salvation?

Day 179: Sha'an (שָׁעַ_ן)

- **Meaning:** To Lean, Rely Upon, Trust

- **Bible Reference:** Proverbs 3:5 – *"Trust in the Lord with all your heart and lean (sha'an) not on your own understanding."*

Message: Sha'an means to lean upon something for support, a reminder that we are not meant to stand alone. Many times, people rely on their own strength, knowledge, or resources instead of fully trusting in God. However, human wisdom is limited, while God's wisdom is infinite. When we **sha'an** on the Lord, we release the pressure of self-sufficiency and rest in His provision. The Bible repeatedly calls us to trust in God rather than in our own understanding. Jesus leaned fully on the Father's will, demonstrating perfect dependence. Are you **sha'an** on God, or are you still trying to carry life's burdens alone?

Reflection Questions for the Day:

1. What does it mean to truly lean on God?

2. Are there areas where you are relying on yourself instead of God?

3. How can you deepen your trust in the Lord daily?

Day 180: Damam (דָּ֫מַ֫ם)

- **Meaning:** To Be Still, Silent, At Rest

- **Bible Reference:** Exodus 14:14 – *"The Lord will fight for you; you need only to be still (damam)."*

Message: Damam teaches us that sometimes, the best response to life's struggles is to be still before God. When the Israelites were trapped between Pharaoh's army and the Red Sea, God commanded them to stop panicking and be still. Silence and stillness allow us to hear God's voice and recognize His power. Many times, we try to fix everything on our own instead of resting in God's ability to fight for us. Jesus demonstrated **damam** when He slept in the storm, knowing the Father was in control. Instead of worrying, we are called to rest in His presence. Are you allowing **damam** to settle your soul, trusting that God is working on your behalf?

Reflection Questions for the Day:

1. Why is it difficult to be still before God?

2. How can practicing stillness strengthen your faith?

3. Are you allowing God to fight for you, or are you trying to fight on your own?

Day 181: Raga (רָ֫גַ֫ע)

- **Meaning:** To Settle, To Bring Peace, To Calm

- **Bible Reference:** Zechariah 9:10 – *"He will proclaim peace to the nations. His rule will extend from sea to sea and from the River to the ends of the earth."*

Message: Raga means to settle or bring calm, describing the peace that comes from God's presence. The world is full of restlessness, but God desires to settle our hearts and minds. Jesus demonstrated **raga** when He calmed the storm with just His word. The disciples were filled with fear, but Jesus showed that true peace is found in trusting Him. When God speaks **raga** over our lives, anxiety, doubt, and turmoil must submit to His authority. The more we abide in Him, the more our hearts are settled. Are you allowing God's **raga** to calm your soul?

Reflection Questions for the Day:

1. What areas of your life need God's calming presence?

2. How can you cultivate a settled heart in uncertain times?

3. Are you seeking peace in the world or in Christ?

Day 182: Selah (סֶ֫לָה)

- **Meaning:** Pause, Meditate, Reflect

- **Bible Reference:** Psalm 46:10 – *"Be still, and know that I am God."*

Message: Selah appears throughout the Psalms, inviting the reader to pause and reflect. In our fast-paced lives, we often rush through moments without stopping to consider God's presence. **Selah** calls us to meditate on His Word, His goodness, and His faithfulness. Jesus often withdrew from the crowds to pray, demonstrating the importance of spiritual reflection. Worship, prayer, and Bible study should not be rushed but should include moments of **selah**, where we pause and listen to God's voice. When we embrace this practice, we experience deeper intimacy with Him. Are you making space for **selah** in your daily life?

Reflection Questions for the Day:

1. How often do you take time to pause and reflect on God's goodness?

2. What distractions keep you from spending quiet time with God?

3. How can you build more intentional moments of **selah** into your daily routine?

Week 26 Conclusion

This week's words reveal that true rest and peace come from God alone. **Menuchah** and **shalom** remind us that God desires wholeness for us. **Noach** and **sha'an** teach us to trust in His comfort and lean on Him. **Damam** and **raga** show us the power of stillness and God's ability to calm every storm. **Selah** calls us to pause, meditate, and dwell in His presence. May we embrace the peace and rest that only He can give, trusting in His perfect care.

Week 27: The Power of Spiritual Growth and Maturity

Day 183: Talmid (תַּ לְ מִ יד)

- **Meaning:** Disciple, Student, Learner
- **Bible Reference:** Matthew 28:19 – *"Go therefore and make disciples (talmidim) of all nations, baptizing them in the name of the Father and of the Son and of the Holy Spirit."*

Message: The word **talmid** refers to a student or disciple who is committed to learning and growing in their faith. Jesus called His followers **talmidim** (disciples), meaning they were not just listeners but dedicated learners who followed His way of life. Being a disciple is more than just believing—it requires active pursuit of God's truth. True discipleship involves studying Scripture, applying it in daily life, and sharing it with others. Jesus taught His disciples not just for knowledge but for transformation and mission. If we are truly His **talmidim**, we will grow in character and commitment to His calling. Are you living as a true **talmid**, learning and growing in Christ daily?

Reflection Questions for the Day:

1. How are you actively growing in your faith as a disciple of Christ?

2. Are you sharing what you've learned with others, as Jesus commanded?

3. What changes can you make to be a more committed **talmid** of Jesus?

Day 184: Binah (בִּ ינָ ה)

- **Meaning:** Understanding, Insight, Discernment

- **Bible Reference:** Proverbs 2:6 – *"For the Lord gives wisdom; from His mouth come knowledge and understanding (binah)."*

Message: Binah is the ability to perceive truth and gain deep spiritual understanding. Many people acquire knowledge, but true wisdom comes from God, who grants discernment to those who seek Him. The Bible warns against leaning on our own understanding but instead trusting in God's **binah**. Jesus demonstrated perfect understanding, always knowing how to respond to challenges and guide others in truth. Spiritual growth requires that we seek God's wisdom in all areas of life. Discernment protects us from deception and helps us make godly decisions. Are you seeking God's **binah**, or are you relying on your own limited understanding?

Reflection Questions for the Day:

1. How do you seek God's wisdom in your daily life?

2. Are there decisions you need to submit to God for greater understanding?

3. How can you develop greater spiritual discernment?

Day 185: Midbar (מ ִדְ בָּ ר)

- **Meaning:** Wilderness, Desert, A Place of Growth

- **Bible Reference:** Hosea 2:14 – *"Therefore, behold, I will allure her, and bring her into the wilderness (midbar), and speak tenderly to her."*

Message: The **midbar** (wilderness) is often seen as a place of dryness, but in the Bible, it is also a place of transformation and spiritual growth. God led Israel through the **midbar** to teach them reliance on Him. Jesus spent forty days in the

193

wilderness preparing for His ministry. Sometimes, God allows us to go through spiritual deserts to deepen our faith and dependence on Him. In the **midbar**, distractions are removed, and we can hear God's voice more clearly. Instead of fearing these seasons, we should embrace them as opportunities for growth. Are you willing to let God shape you in the **midbar** of life?

Reflection Questions for the Day:

1. Have you experienced a wilderness season in your faith?

2. How can you embrace these seasons as opportunities for growth?

3. What lessons have you learned during times of spiritual dryness?

Day 186: Yatsar (יָצַר)

- **Meaning:** To Form, Shape, Mold

- **Bible Reference:** Isaiah 64:8 – *"Yet You, Lord, are our Father. We are the clay, You are the potter; we are all the work of Your hand."*

Message: Yatsar refers to the process of forming and molding something, just as a potter shapes clay. God is the ultimate Potter, shaping us into the people He desires us to be. Spiritual growth requires allowing Him to **yatsar** us, even when the process is difficult. Trials, challenges, and corrections are part of this molding. Just as clay must be softened and shaped before it becomes useful, our hearts must be yielded to God's touch. The more we submit to His shaping, the more we reflect Christ's character. Are you allowing God to **yatsar** your life, or are you resisting His hand?

Reflection Questions for the Day:

1. How has God been shaping your character recently?

2. Are you allowing yourself to be molded, or are you resisting?

3. What steps can you take to be more flexible to God's work in your life?

Day 187: Machazik (מַ_חֲ_זִ_יק)

- **Meaning:** Strengthen, Encourage, Hold Firm

- **Bible Reference:** Joshua 1:9 – *"Be strong (machazik) and courageous. Do not be afraid; do not be discouraged, for the Lord your God will be with you wherever you go."*

Message: To **machazik** means to strengthen, encourage, and take hold of something firmly. Joshua was commanded to be **machazik**—strong and courageous—because God was with him. Spiritual growth requires perseverance, even when challenges arise. We gain strength not from ourselves but from God, who empowers us to walk in faith. Encouraging others and being encouraged is essential for growth in the body of Christ. Jesus told His disciples to take heart because He had overcome the world, reminding us to stand firm. Are you being **machazik** in your faith, standing strong in God's promises?

Reflection Questions for the Day:

1. How do you stay strong in faith during difficult times?

2. Are you surrounding yourself with people who encourage your spiritual growth?

3. How can you encourage someone else in their faith this week?

Day 188: Eder (עֵדֶר)

- **Meaning:** Flock, Community, Fellowship

- **Bible Reference:** Acts 2:42 – *"They devoted themselves to the apostles' teaching and to fellowship (eder), to the breaking of bread and to prayer."*

Message: Eder refers to a flock or a gathered community. Just as sheep need a shepherd, believers need spiritual fellowship and guidance. God never intended for us to grow spiritually in isolation. The early church thrived because they were committed to **eder**, building strong relationships in faith. Growth happens when we encourage, correct, and walk alongside one another. Jesus, the Good Shepherd, calls us into His **eder**, caring for us and teaching us to care for one another. Are you actively engaging in spiritual community, or are you trying to grow alone?

Reflection Questions for the Day:

1. How has being part of a faith community helped your spiritual growth?

2. Are you investing in relationships that strengthen your faith?

3. How can you be more involved in encouraging and helping others in their faith journey?

Day 189: Tsama (צָמֵא)

- **Meaning:** Thirst, Deep Desire, Longing

- **Bible Reference:** Psalm 42:1 – *"As the deer pants for streams of water, so my soul thirsts (tsama) for You, my God."*

Message: Tsama describes an intense longing and thirst for God's presence. Just as the body needs water to survive, our souls need God for true fulfillment. Many people try to satisfy their **tsama** with temporary things, but only God can quench the deep thirst of the soul. Jesus promised living water to those who come to Him, offering satisfaction that the world cannot provide. True spiritual growth happens when we cultivate a hunger for God's Word and His presence. The more we seek Him, the more we are filled. Are you thirsting for God, or are you settling for lesser things?

Reflection Questions for the Day:

1. What are you longing for most in your life right now?

2. How can you deepen your thirst for God's presence?

3. What distractions might be keeping you from fully pursuing God?

Week 27 Conclusion

This week's words emphasize the journey of growing in faith. **Talmid** reminds us to be lifelong learners, while **binah** gives us the wisdom to grow deeper. **Midbar** teaches that even spiritual deserts can bring growth, and **yatsar** shows that God is shaping us for His purpose. **Machazik** strengthens us, **eder** reminds us of the importance of community, and **tsama** calls us to long for more of God. Spiritual growth is a lifelong process, but when we trust God, He leads us into deeper maturity and purpose.

197

Week 28: The Power of God's Covenant and Promises

Day 190: Berit (בְּ ר ית)

- **Meaning:** Covenant, Agreement, Divine Promise

- **Bible Reference:** Genesis 17:7 – *"I will establish My covenant (berit) as an everlasting covenant between Me and you and your descendants after you for the generations to come, to be your God and the God of your descendants after you."*

Message: A **berit** is a sacred agreement between God and His people. Throughout Scripture, God made covenants with Noah, Abraham, Moses, and David, each revealing His faithfulness. Unlike human contracts, which depend on both parties fulfilling their roles, God's **berit** is built on His unwavering promises. The ultimate **berit** was fulfilled through Jesus, whose sacrifice established the New Covenant of grace. Because of His **berit**, we have access to eternal life, forgiveness, and a relationship with Him. Knowing we are part of God's covenant brings security and assurance in His unchanging love. Are you living in the confidence of God's **berit**, trusting His promises?

Reflection Questions for the Day:

1. How does understanding God's covenant deepen your faith?

2. Are you fully embracing the New Covenant through Jesus?

3. What does God's faithfulness in His **berit** mean for your daily life?

Day 191: Emunah (אֱ מוּנ ָה)

- **Meaning:** Faith, Steadfastness, Trustworthiness

- **Bible Reference:** Habakkuk 2:4 – *"The righteous will live by his faith (emunah)."*

Message: Emunah is not just believing in God—it is a steadfast trust in His promises and character. True faith endures hardships and remains unwavering even when circumstances seem uncertain. Abraham demonstrated **emunah** when he trusted God's promise of a son despite his old age. Jesus called His followers to have faith that moves mountains, showing that **emunah** brings divine power into our lives. When we rely on God's **emunah**, we find peace and confidence in His plans. Faith is the foundation of our relationship with God and the key to receiving His promises. Are you living with unwavering **emunah**, trusting God fully?

Reflection Questions for the Day:

1. What challenges have tested your faith recently?

2. How can you strengthen your **emunah** in God's promises?

3. Are you trusting God's faithfulness even when answers are delayed?

Day 192: Zakar (זָ֫כַר)

- **Meaning:** To Remember, To Recall, To Keep in Mind

- **Bible Reference:** Deuteronomy 8:18 – *"But remember (zakar) the Lord your God, for it is He who gives you the ability to produce wealth."*

Message: Zakar is the act of remembering God's faithfulness and His past works. Throughout Scripture, God repeatedly tells His people to **zakar** His mighty deeds, ensuring that they do not forget His promises. Forgetting leads to doubt and disobedience, but remembering strengthens faith. The Israelites built altars and celebrated feasts to **zakar** God's deliverance and provision. Jesus instituted communion as a way to **zakar** His sacrifice, keeping our hearts aligned with Him. When we **zakar** God's goodness, our trust in Him deepens. Are you intentionally remembering God's faithfulness, or are you forgetting His past provisions?

Reflection Questions for the Day:

1. How has God been faithful to you in the past?

2. What practical ways can you remind yourself of God's promises daily?

3. How does remembering God's faithfulness strengthen your trust in Him?

Day 193: Chesed (חֶ֫סֶד)

- **Meaning:** Loving-kindness, Covenant Mercy, Unfailing Love

- **Bible Reference:** Lamentations 3:22 – *"Because of the Lord's great love (chesed) we are not consumed, for His compassions never fail."*

Message: Chesed is God's steadfast, unfailing love that remains constant despite human failure. His **chesed** is the foundation of His covenant, ensuring that His love and mercy never waver. Even when Israel turned away, God's **chesed** remained, calling them back to Him. Jesus' sacrifice on the cross is the ultimate demonstration of **chesed**, securing our redemption. We are called to reflect His **chesed** in our relationships, extending mercy and kindness to others. Understanding God's **chesed** transforms how we view Him—

He is not just a judge but a loving Father. Are you fully receiving and reflecting God's **chesed** in your life?

Reflection Questions for the Day:

1. How have you personally experienced God's **chesed**?

2. In what ways can you reflect God's loving-kindness to others?

3. Are you resting in the security of God's unfailing love?

Day 194: Kahal (קָהַל)

- **Meaning:** Assembly, Congregation, Called-out People

- **Bible Reference:** Psalm 22:22 – *"I will declare Your name to my people; in the assembly (kahal) I will praise You."*

Message: Kahal refers to the assembly of God's people, emphasizing the importance of spiritual community. In the Old Testament, Israel was God's **kahal**, gathered to worship and follow His laws. In the New Testament, the Church is the new **kahal**, called to be Christ's body on earth. Being part of a **kahal** provides encouragement, accountability, and shared faith. God's promises are often fulfilled through community, not isolation. Jesus said that where two or more are gathered in His name, He is present among them. Are you actively engaging in God's **kahal**, building up His people?

Reflection Questions for the Day:

1. How important is spiritual community in your life?

2. Are you actively contributing to your church or faith group?

3. How can you strengthen your connection with God's **kahal**?

Day 195: Shamar (שָׁ מַ ר)

- **Meaning:** To Keep, To Guard, To Preserve

- **Bible Reference:** Deuteronomy 11:1 – *"Love the Lord your God and keep (shamar) His requirements, His decrees, His laws, and His commands always."*

Message: To **shamar** means to guard and protect something valuable. God commands us to **shamar** His Word, treasuring it in our hearts and obeying it. Throughout the Bible, God calls His people to **shamar** His covenant, remaining faithful to Him. When we **shamar** His commands, we walk in His blessings and avoid unnecessary struggles. Jesus reminded His followers to **shamar** His teachings, demonstrating love through obedience. The enemy constantly tries to steal God's truth from our hearts, so we must be diligent in guarding it. Are you faithfully **shamar** God's Word, keeping it at the center of your life?

Reflection Questions for the Day:

1. How do you guard God's truth in your heart?

2. Are you actively obeying and keeping God's commandments?

3. What distractions might be pulling you away from **shamar** His Word?

Day 196: Go'el (גּוֹ אֵ ל)

- **Meaning:** Redeemer, Deliverer, One Who Saves

- **Bible Reference:** Job 19:25 – *"I know that my Redeemer (go'el) lives, and that in the end He will stand on the earth."*

Message: A **go'el** was a redeemer, someone who rescued family members from slavery or restored lost inheritance. Boaz acted as Ruth's **go'el**, securing her future. Jesus is our ultimate **go'el**, redeeming us from sin and death through His sacrifice. His redemption is not partial—it is complete, restoring what was lost and bringing us into full relationship with God. Because of our **go'el**, we are no longer bound by our past but free to walk in new life. Redemption is a gift we could never earn but must fully embrace. Are you living in the freedom that your **go'el** has secured for you?

Reflection Questions for the Day:

1. What does Jesus' role as your **go'el** mean to you?

2. Are you still living in bondage to sin, or are you embracing redemption?

3. How can you share the message of redemption with others?

Week 28 Conclusion

This week's words highlight the unshakable foundation of God's promises. **Berit** reminds us of His eternal covenant, while **emunah** calls us to trust in His faithfulness. **Zakar** urges us to remember His past works, and **chesed** reveals His steadfast love. **Kahal** emphasizes the importance of community, and **shamar** teaches us to guard His truth. Finally, **go'el** reassures us of Jesus' redeeming power. God's promises never fail, securing our faith and future in Him.

Week 29: The Power of God's Wisdom and Instruction

Day 197: Chokmah (חָכְמָה)

- **Meaning:** Wisdom, Skill, Godly Understanding

- **Bible Reference:** Proverbs 9:10 – *"The fear of the Lord is the beginning of wisdom (chokmah), and knowledge of the Holy One is understanding."*

Message: Chokmah is more than intelligence; it is wisdom that comes from God. The Bible teaches that wisdom begins with the fear of the Lord—reverence and respect for Him. Solomon asked for **chokmah**, knowing that true success depends on God's guidance. The world offers many forms of knowledge, but only divine **chokmah** leads to righteousness and lasting impact. Jesus embodied perfect wisdom, teaching with authority and insight that confounded even the most learned men. When we seek God's **chokmah**, we receive discernment, clarity, and the ability to make godly decisions. Are you relying on God's wisdom, or are you trusting in your own understanding?

Reflection Questions for the Day:

1. How do you actively seek God's wisdom in your life?

2. Are you making decisions based on **chokmah**, or worldly knowledge?

3. How can you grow in godly wisdom daily?

Day 198: Da'at (דַּעַת)

- **Meaning:** Knowledge, Awareness, Understanding

- **Bible Reference:** Proverbs 2:6 – *"For the Lord gives wisdom; from His mouth come knowledge (da'at) and understanding."*

Message: Da'at represents knowledge that comes from God, not just human learning. Many people pursue knowledge but lack the spiritual insight that comes from knowing God. The Bible warns that knowledge without love or humility can lead to pride. True **da'at** comes from a relationship with God, where He reveals truth to His people. Jesus spoke in parables, giving knowledge to those with hearts open to Him. When we seek **da'at**, we grow in our understanding of His ways. Are you seeking knowledge that leads to pride, or **da'at** that leads to a deeper relationship with God?

Reflection Questions for the Day:

1. How can you differentiate between worldly knowledge and godly **da'at**?

2. What steps can you take to grow in the knowledge of God?

3. Are you using your knowledge to glorify God or for selfish gain?

Day 199: Binah (בִּינָה)

- **Meaning:** Discernment, Insight, Understanding Beyond Surface Level

- **Bible Reference:** Proverbs 4:7 – *"The beginning of wisdom is this: Get wisdom. Though it cost all you have, get understanding (binah)."*

Message: Binah is the ability to understand beyond the surface, seeing the deeper meaning of things. It is a key part of wisdom, helping us make decisions that align with God's will. While **da'at** is knowledge and **chokmah** is wisdom, **binah** is the insight to apply both correctly. Solomon sought **binah** to lead Israel with justice and righteousness. Jesus demonstrated **binah** in every conversation, knowing people's hearts beyond their words. Developing **binah** requires spending time with God, meditating on His Word, and seeking the Holy Spirit's guidance. Are you asking God for **binah** to navigate life with discernment?

Reflection Questions for the Day:

1. How do you seek God's discernment in your daily decisions?

2. What is an example of a time when you needed deeper insight?

3. How can you train yourself to think with **binah**?

Day 200: Musar (מוּסָר)

- **Meaning:** Instruction, Discipline, Correction

- **Bible Reference:** Proverbs 3:11 – *"My son, do not despise the Lord's discipline (musar), and do not resent His rebuke."*

Message: Musar refers to instruction and discipline that leads to wisdom and growth. God, like a loving Father, disciplines His children to guide them into righteousness. Though correction can be uncomfortable, it is a sign of God's care and commitment to our spiritual maturity. Proverbs is full of teachings on **musar**, showing that those who embrace discipline gain wisdom. Jesus corrected His disciples, not to condemn them, but to refine their character. When we accept **musar**, we become stronger, wiser, and more aligned with God's will. Are you resisting correction, or are you allowing God's **musar** to shape you?

Reflection Questions for the Day:

1. How do you respond to God's correction?

2. Are there areas where God is disciplining you to grow?

3. How can you embrace **musar** as a path to wisdom?

Day 201: Yirah (יִ ר אָה)

- **Meaning:** Fear of the Lord, Awe, Reverence

- **Bible Reference:** Psalm 111:10 – *"The fear (yirah) of the Lord is the beginning of wisdom; all who follow His precepts have good understanding."*

Message: Yirah is not fear in the sense of terror, but a deep reverence for God's holiness and authority. The Bible teaches that wisdom begins with **yirah**, recognizing that God is supreme. This kind of fear leads to obedience, humility, and trust in His ways. Many people lack **yirah**, treating God casually rather than with honor. Jesus, though the Son of God, walked in perfect **yirah**, submitting fully to the Father's will. When we develop **yirah**, we align our hearts with God's purposes. Are you living with a reverent fear of the Lord, or are you treating Him lightly?

Reflection Questions for the Day:

1. What does it mean to fear the Lord in a healthy way?

2. How does **yirah** lead to deeper wisdom?

3. Are there areas where you need to develop a greater reverence for God?

Day 202: Lev Tov (לֵ ב טוֹב)

- **Meaning:** A Good Heart, A Wise and Kind Spirit

- **Bible Reference:** Proverbs 4:23 – *"Above all else, guard your heart (lev tov), for everything you do flows from it."*

Message: A **lev tov** is a heart that seeks wisdom, kindness, and righteousness. In the Bible, the heart represents the center of one's thoughts, emotions, and decisions. A wise heart is not just about knowledge but about choosing goodness and integrity in all things. Jesus described the pure in heart as those who will see God, showing the importance of inner transformation. When our **lev tov** is aligned with God's wisdom, our actions reflect His character. The more we guard our hearts against sin and pride, the more we grow spiritually. Is your **lev tov** centered on God's wisdom, or is it distracted by worldly desires?

Reflection Questions for the Day:

1. How do you cultivate a heart that reflects God's wisdom?

2. Are there things in your heart that need to be surrendered to God?

3. How can you show a **lev tov** in your relationships?

Day 203: Sekhel (שֵׂ כֶ ל)

- **Meaning:** Prudence, Intelligence, Common Sense
- **Bible Reference:** Proverbs 19:11 – *"A person's wisdom (sekhel) yields patience; it is to one's glory to overlook an offense."*

Message: Sekhel is practical wisdom—knowing how to apply knowledge in daily life. It includes common sense, good judgment, and patience. The Bible warns that knowledge without **sekhel** leads to arrogance and poor choices. Jesus often used simple, practical teachings to guide people in wise living. Many people seek spiritual wisdom but neglect the everyday **sekhel** that helps them live righteously. When we develop **sekhel**, we make decisions that reflect God's wisdom and bring peace to our lives. Are you using godly **sekhel** in your daily actions and interactions?

Reflection Questions for the Day:

1. How can you grow in practical wisdom?

2. Are there areas where you need to apply more patience and prudence?

3. How does **sekhel** help you live a life that honors God?

Week 29 Conclusion

This week's words highlight different aspects of wisdom. **Chokmah** teaches us godly wisdom, while **da'at** and **binah** deepen our understanding. **Musar** reminds us that discipline leads to growth, and **yirah** calls us to reverence God. **Lev tov** teaches us that wisdom begins in the heart, and **sekhel** shows us how to apply it in daily life. Walking in wisdom is a lifelong journey, but with God's guidance, we grow in discernment, faith, and spiritual maturity.

Week 30: The Power of Spiritual Renewal and Transformation

Day 204: Chadesh (חָדֵשׁ)

- **Meaning:** To Renew, To Restore, To Make New

- **Bible Reference:** Isaiah 40:31 – *"But those who hope in the Lord will renew (chadesh) their strength."*

Message: Chadesh signifies the process of spiritual renewal and restoration. Life can be exhausting, but God promises to **chadesh** our strength when we trust in Him. Renewal is not just about physical restoration; it is about refreshing our souls through prayer, worship, and reliance on God. The Bible frequently speaks of renewal—new mercies every morning, a new heart, and a new covenant through Christ. Jesus came to **chadesh** our lives, making all things new. When we allow God to renew us, we experience His joy, strength, and purpose in a fresh way. Are you seeking God's renewal daily, or are you running on empty?

Reflection Questions for the Day:

1. What areas of your life need spiritual renewal?

2. How can you invite God to refresh and restore you?

3. Are you making time for the practices that bring **chadesh** into your life?

Day 205: Lev Chadash (לֵב חָדָשׁ)

- **Meaning:** A New Heart, Transformed Inner Being

- **Bible Reference:** Ezekiel 36:26 – *"I will give you a new heart (lev chadash) and put a new spirit in you."*

Message: Lev chadash is the promise of a transformed heart, given by God to those who surrender to Him. Our natural hearts are prone to sin, selfishness, and hardness toward

God's ways. However, God does not merely fix our old hearts—He gives us **lev chadash**, a completely new and purified heart. Through the Holy Spirit, we are changed from the inside out, becoming more like Christ. Spiritual transformation is a process, but as we yield to God, He shapes our desires, thoughts, and actions. A **lev chadash** leads to a life that reflects His love, holiness, and purpose. Are you allowing God to give you a **lev chadash**, or are you holding onto your old ways?

Reflection Questions for the Day:

1. How does having a new heart change your relationship with God?

2. Are there areas in your life where you need inner transformation?

3. What steps can you take to cultivate a **lev chadash**?

Day 206: Qadosh (קָדוֹשׁ)

- **Meaning:** Holy, Set Apart, Sacred

- **Bible Reference:** Leviticus 11:44 – *"I am the Lord your God; consecrate yourselves and be holy (qadosh), because I am holy."*

Message: Qadosh means to be set apart for God's purposes. Holiness is not about perfection but about being devoted to God and living according to His ways. Throughout Scripture, God calls His people to be **qadosh**, reflecting His character to the world. Jesus, as the ultimate example of holiness, lived in perfect obedience to the Father. When we pursue **qadosh**, we reject the things that pull us away from God and embrace His truth. Living a holy life requires daily choices, relying on the

215

Holy Spirit's guidance. Are you striving to be **qadosh**, set apart for God's glory?

Reflection Questions for the Day:

1. What does it mean to be set apart for God?

2. Are there things in your life that hinder your pursuit of holiness?

3. How can you grow in your commitment to being **qadosh**?

Day 207: Shuv (שׁוּב)

- **Meaning:** To Return, To Repent, To Turn Back

- **Bible Reference:** Joel 2:13 – *"Return (shuv) to the Lord your God, for He is gracious and compassionate."*

Message: Shuv is the act of turning back to God, a call to repentance and restoration. The Bible repeatedly urges God's people to **shuv** from sin and seek His presence. Repentance is not just about feeling sorry but about a genuine change of heart and direction. The prodigal son in Jesus' parable demonstrated true **shuv**, turning away from his old life and returning to his father. God is always ready to receive us when we **shuv**, no matter how far we have wandered. Transformation begins with repentance, aligning our hearts with God's will. Are you willing to **shuv**, turning away from anything that separates you from God?

Reflection Questions for the Day:

1. What areas of your life need repentance and redirection?

216

2. How can you practice daily repentance as a way of spiritual renewal?

3. Are you truly turning back to God, or just acknowledging your sins without change?

Day 208: Hit'chadeshut (הֱתְחַדְּשׁוּת)

- **Meaning:** Renewal, Revival, Spiritual Awakening

- **Bible Reference:** Romans 12:2 – *"Be transformed by the renewing (hit'chadeshut) of your mind."*

Message: Hit'chadeshut is the ongoing process of spiritual renewal and revival. Transformation does not happen overnight but requires daily surrender to God's work in us. Paul calls believers to renew their minds, replacing worldly thinking with God's truth. This renewal affects our actions, decisions, and how we see ourselves in Christ. True **hit'chadeshut** leads to a deeper relationship with God and a passion for His kingdom. Revival begins in the heart before it spreads outward. Are you seeking daily **hit'chadeshut**, allowing God to shape you continually?

Reflection Questions for the Day:

1. How can you renew your mind in God's Word daily?

2. What habits need to change for true spiritual transformation?

3. Are you experiencing revival in your heart, or are you spiritually stagnant?

Day 209: Taharah (טֳהֳרָה)

- **Meaning:** Purity, Cleansing, Spiritual Cleanliness

- **Bible Reference:** Psalm 51:10 – *"Create in me a pure (taharah) heart, O God, and renew a steadfast spirit within me."*

Message: Taharah is the state of spiritual purity and cleansing before God. In the Old Testament, purification rituals symbolized the need for spiritual cleanliness. Jesus taught that external rituals are meaningless if the heart is impure. True **taharah** comes from allowing God to cleanse us from sin and renew our hearts. Living a life of purity is about aligning our thoughts, actions, and desires with God's holiness. The Holy Spirit sanctifies us, helping us grow in purity. Are you actively pursuing **taharah**, keeping your heart clean before God?

Reflection Questions for the Day:

1. What does spiritual purity mean in your daily life?

2. Are there things in your life that are contaminating your heart?

3. How can you walk in greater purity and holiness?

Day 210: Tikun (תּ. קוּן)

- **Meaning:** Restoration, Repair, Fixing What is Broken

- **Bible Reference:** Isaiah 58:12 – *"You will be called Repairer of Broken Walls, Restorer (tikun) of Streets with Dwellings."*

Message: Tikun refers to restoring what is broken, bringing healing and renewal. Sin has damaged humanity, but God's plan has always been about **tikun**—redemption and restoration. Jesus came to **tikun** our broken relationship with God, making a way for reconciliation. As His followers, we are called to be agents of **tikun,** bringing healing to the world around us. This includes restoring relationships, helping the needy, and sharing the gospel. Our personal transformation is part of the greater work of **tikun** that God is doing in the world. Are you partnering with God in His mission of restoration?

Reflection Questions for the Day:

1. What areas of your life need restoration?

2. How can you be part of God's work of **tikun** in the world?

3. Are you allowing God to heal and restore you completely?

Week 30 Conclusion

This week's words remind us of the transformative power of God. **Chadesh** and **lev chadash** show that renewal begins with God's work in our hearts. **Qadosh** and **taharah** call us to holiness and purity. **Shuv** and **hit'chadeshut** emphasize the importance of repentance and daily renewal, while **tikun** reveals God's ultimate plan to restore all things. Spiritual transformation is a lifelong journey, but as we walk with God, He makes us new.

Week 31: The Power of God's Deliverance and Victory

Day 211: Yeshuah (יְשׁוּעָה)

- **Meaning:** Salvation, Deliverance, Rescue

- **Bible Reference:** Psalm 62:1 – *"Truly my soul finds rest in God; my salvation (yeshuah) comes from Him."*

Message: Yeshuah means salvation, not just in the sense of eternal life but also deliverance from troubles, sin, and oppression. The name "Jesus" (Yeshua) comes from this word, signifying that He is the ultimate source of our salvation. Throughout the Old Testament, God repeatedly provided **yeshuah** to His people, rescuing them from slavery, enemies, and judgment. Salvation is more than a moment; it is an ongoing work of God in our lives. Jesus' sacrifice on the cross secured our **yeshuah**, setting us free from sin and bringing us into eternal life. We are called to trust in God's **yeshuah**, knowing He is always our deliverer. Are you living in the fullness of the **yeshuah** God has provided?

Reflection Questions for the Day:

1. What does salvation mean to you beyond just eternal life?

2. How have you seen God's deliverance in your life?

3. Are you walking in the freedom that comes with God's **yeshuah**?

Day 212: Padah (פָּדָה)

- **Meaning:** To Redeem, To Ransom, To Set Free

- **Bible Reference:** Psalm 34:22 – *"The Lord will rescue (padah) His servants; no one who takes refuge in Him will be condemned."*

Message: Padah refers to the act of redemption, paying a price to set someone free. In ancient times, a person could be redeemed from slavery by a relative or benefactor. Jesus is our ultimate **padah**, who paid the price for our sins with His own blood. Redemption is not just about being saved from something but being saved for something—a restored relationship with God and a life of purpose. The Israelites were redeemed from Egypt, but many failed to walk in the freedom God provided. True redemption means embracing the new life that God has given us. Are you living as someone who has been **padah**, fully redeemed and set free?

Reflection Questions for the Day:

1. What does it mean to be redeemed by God?

2. How does Christ's redemption change how you live today?

3. Are you walking in the freedom that His **padah** provides?

Day 213: Matzil (מַ‏צִ‏יל)

- **Meaning:** Deliverer, Rescuer, Savior

- **Bible Reference:** 2 Samuel 22:2 – *"The Lord is my rock, my fortress, and my deliverer (matzil)."*

Message: Matzil describes someone who rescues or delivers from danger. God is often called a **matzil** in the Bible, as He repeatedly rescued His people from enemies and hardship. David called God his **matzil**, recognizing that his victories were not by his own strength but by God's power. Jesus is our ultimate **matzil**, delivering us from sin and death. Even today, God continues to act as our **matzil**, saving us from situations we cannot escape on our own. Trusting in Him means recognizing that He is always fighting for us. Are you relying on God as your **matzil**, or are you trying to rescue yourself?

Reflection Questions for the Day:

1. When have you experienced God's deliverance in your life?

2. Do you fully trust God to be your **matzil**, or do you try to solve things on your own?

3. How can you remind yourself of God's power to rescue you?

Day 214: Nachal (נָ_חַ_ל)

- **Meaning:** To Possess, To Inherit, To Receive as a Gift

- **Bible Reference:** Deuteronomy 4:20 – *"But as for you, the Lord took you and brought you out of the iron-smelting furnace, out of Egypt, to be the people of His inheritance (nachal), as you are now."*

Message: Nachal means to inherit or receive something valuable. God's people were promised an inheritance, not because of their efforts but because of His grace. The Israelites were given the Promised Land as a **nachal**, yet they had to trust God to take hold of it. As believers, we are heirs of God's kingdom, receiving salvation, righteousness, and eternal life as our **nachal**. Too often, we fail to claim the inheritance God has given us, living below the promises He has made. When we walk in faith, we step into our **nachal** with confidence. Are you embracing your spiritual inheritance, or are you settling for less than what God has promised?

Reflection Questions for the Day:

1. What spiritual inheritance has God given you?

2. Are you living as an heir of God's kingdom?

3. How can you walk in the fullness of your **nachal**?

Day 215: Kalah (כָּלָה)

- **Meaning:** To Complete, To Finish, To Fulfill

- **Bible Reference:** John 19:30 – *"Jesus said, 'It is finished (kalah).' With that, He bowed His head and gave up His spirit."*

Message: Kalah is a powerful word that signifies the completion of something. When Jesus declared "It is finished," He was announcing that His work of redemption was complete. God always finishes what He starts—His promises are not left unfulfilled. The Bible reminds us that He who began a good work in us will **kalah** it to completion. Too often, we start strong in faith but struggle to persevere. But God's strength allows us to finish well. Are you trusting that God will **kalah** His work in your life, bringing it to full completion?

Reflection Questions for the Day:

1. What does Jesus' finished work on the cross mean for you?

2. Are you persevering in your faith, trusting God to complete His work in you?

3. How can you rely on God's strength to **kalah** what He has started?

Day 216: Gibbor (גִּבּוֹר)

- **Meaning:** Mighty, Warrior, Champion

- **Bible Reference:** Isaiah 9:6 – *"And He will be called Wonderful Counselor, Mighty God (El Gibbor), Everlasting Father, Prince of Peace."*

Message: Gibbor describes one who is strong, courageous, and victorious. God is often called **El Gibbor**, the Mighty God, who fights for His people. In the Bible, warriors like David, Gideon, and Joshua were **gibbor** because they relied on God's strength, not their own. Jesus is our ultimate **Gibbor**, defeating sin, death, and the powers of darkness. We, too, are called to be spiritual warriors, clothed in God's armor and standing firm in faith. Victory comes not from our strength but from surrender to the **Gibbor** who fights for us. Are you trusting in God's might, or are you trying to fight your battles alone?

Reflection Questions for the Day:

1. How do you see God as a warrior in your life?

2. Are you standing firm in faith, trusting in His strength?

3. How can you walk in victory through the power of **El Gibbor**?

Week 31 Conclusion

This week's words remind us of God's mighty power to deliver and give us victory. **Yeshuah** assures us of salvation, while **padah** speaks of the price Jesus paid for our freedom. **Matzil** reveals God as our rescuer, and **nachal** reminds us of the inheritance He has given us. **Kalah** confirms that God's work is always completed, and **gibbor** declares Him as the

Mighty Warrior who fights for us. When we trust in God's deliverance, we walk in freedom, confidence, and victory.

Week 32: The Power of God's Presence

Day 217: Shekinah (שְׁכִינָה)

- **Meaning:** Dwelling, Divine Presence, Glory of God

- **Bible Reference:** Exodus 40:34 – *"Then the cloud covered the tent of meeting, and the glory of the Lord (Shekinah) filled the tabernacle."*

Message: Shekinah refers to the manifest presence of God dwelling among His people. In the Old Testament, God's **Shekinah** was seen in the cloud by day and the fire by night, guiding Israel. His presence filled the tabernacle and later the temple, signifying His nearness. In the New Testament, Jesus embodied the **Shekinah** of God, dwelling among humanity. Through the Holy Spirit, God's presence now dwells within every believer. Experiencing **Shekinah** transforms us, drawing us closer to God's heart. Are you making room for God's **Shekinah** to dwell in your life daily?

Reflection Questions for the Day:

1. How do you experience God's presence in your life?

2. Are there distractions keeping you from dwelling in His **Shekinah**?

3. How can you create a life that welcomes God's presence daily?

Day 218: Panim (פָּנִים)

- **Meaning:** Face, Presence, Before God

- **Bible Reference:** Exodus 33:14 – *"The Lord replied, 'My Presence (Panim) will go with you, and I will give you rest.'"*

Message: **Panim** means "face" and is often used in Scripture to describe being in God's presence. Moses sought to see God's **Panim**, longing for deeper intimacy with Him. The Bible calls us to seek God's **Panim**, living in constant awareness of His presence. Sin separates us from God's **Panim**, but through Christ, we are restored to face-to-face relationship with Him. When we live before His **Panim**, our lives are guided by His wisdom and peace. Worship and prayer bring us closer to His **Panim**, renewing our hearts. Are you seeking God's **Panim**, longing to dwell in His presence daily?

Reflection Questions for the Day:

1. How can you seek God's **Panim** more intentionally?

2. What keeps you from experiencing God's presence fully?

3. How does living before His face change your daily life?

Day 219: Ruach (רוּחַ)

- **Meaning:** Spirit, Wind, Breath

- **Bible Reference:** Genesis 1:2 – *"Now the earth was formless and empty, darkness was over the surface of the deep, and the Spirit (Ruach) of God was hovering over the waters."*

Message: **Ruach** is the breath of God, the Spirit that gives life and power. In creation, God's **Ruach** moved over the waters, bringing order and life. In the New Testament, Jesus breathed on His disciples, filling them with the Holy Spirit. The **Ruach** of God empowers believers, giving them wisdom, strength, and spiritual gifts. Without His Spirit, our lives are lifeless and powerless. The more we yield to the **Ruach**, the more we walk in the fullness of God's presence. Are you allowing God's **Ruach** to move in and through your life?

Reflection Questions for the Day:

1. How do you experience the Holy Spirit's work in your life?

2. Are you making space for the **Ruach** to move in you?

3. What steps can you take to walk more in the Spirit?

Day 220: Yashab (יָשַׁב)

- **Meaning:** To Dwell, To Sit, To Remain
- **Bible Reference:** Psalm 91:1 – *"Whoever dwells (Yashab) in the shelter of the Most High will rest in the shadow of the Almighty."*

Message: Yashab speaks of abiding in God's presence, not just visiting Him occasionally. Many people seek God only in times of trouble, but He calls us to **yashab**—to dwell with Him daily. Jesus taught that those who abide in Him will bear much fruit, showing the importance of constant fellowship with God. Dwelling in God's presence provides peace, security, and strength. Just as a home provides shelter and rest, God's presence becomes our true dwelling place. When we **yashab**, we cultivate a deeper relationship with Him. Are you dwelling in God's presence daily, or just visiting occasionally?

Reflection Questions for the Day:

1. What does it mean to truly dwell in God's presence?

2. Are you consistently spending time in His presence, or only when needed?

3. How can you develop a habit of abiding in Him daily?

Day 221: Makom (מָקוֹם)

- **Meaning:** Place, Dwelling, Sacred Space

- **Bible Reference:** Genesis 28:16 – *"Surely the Lord is in this place (Makom), and I was not aware of it."*

Message: Makom means "place" but is often used to describe the presence of God. When Jacob encountered God in a dream, he recognized that he was in a sacred **Makom**. The temple in Jerusalem was a holy **Makom**, where God's glory was revealed. Today, through Christ, we become God's **Makom**, His dwelling place. Every space we enter can become a **Makom** of worship if we acknowledge His presence. When we create sacred spaces in our hearts and lives, we experience deeper intimacy with Him. Are you making space for God to be the **Makom** in your life?

Reflection Questions for the Day:

1. How do you recognize God's presence in everyday places?

2. Are you setting apart sacred time and space for God in your life?

3. How can you turn your home, work, and daily routines into a **Makom** for God?

Day 222: Shakan (שָׁכַ_ן)

- **Meaning:** To Settle, To Dwell, To Abide Permanently

- **Bible Reference:** Psalm 37:3 – *"Trust in the Lord and do good; dwell (Shakan) in the land and enjoy safe pasture."*

Message: Shakan goes beyond temporary presence—it means to settle and abide permanently. God did not just visit His people; He **shakan** among them. In the New Testament, Jesus "tabernacled" among us, demonstrating God's desire for close relationship. The Holy Spirit now **shakan** within every believer, making our hearts His home. This abiding presence brings security, guidance, and strength. The more we embrace God's **shakan**, the more we experience His peace. Are you letting God fully **shakan** in your life, or are you holding back areas from Him?

Reflection Questions for the Day:

1. What does it mean for God to dwell permanently in your life?

2. Are you allowing the Holy Spirit to fully settle in your heart?

3. How can you build a lifestyle of constant communion with God?

Day 223: Niglah (נ.ג.ל.ה)

- **Meaning:** To Reveal, To Make Known, To Unveil

- **Bible Reference:** Isaiah 40:5 – *"And the glory of the Lord will be revealed (Niglah), and all people will see it together."*

Message: Niglah speaks of God unveiling His presence and truth. Throughout history, God has revealed Himself in powerful ways—through visions, signs, and ultimately through Jesus. Revelation is not just about knowledge but experiencing God personally. When we seek Him with open hearts, He makes Himself known. The more time we spend in His presence, the more He **niglah** His wisdom and direction to us. God is not distant; He desires to reveal Himself to those who seek Him. Are you seeking God's **niglah**, allowing Him to reveal His presence and truth in your life?

Reflection Questions for the Day:

1. How has God revealed Himself to you in your spiritual journey?

2. Are you actively seeking to know Him more deeply?

3. What steps can you take to be more aware of His presence?

Week 32 Conclusion

This week's words highlight the depth of God's presence in our lives. **Shekinah** reveals His glory, while **Panim** calls us to seek His face. **Ruach** reminds us of His Spirit, and **Yashab** teaches us to dwell with Him. **Makom** shows that every place can be sacred, and **Shakan** confirms His desire to abide permanently. **Niglah** assures us that God reveals Himself to those who seek Him. Living in God's presence transforms our hearts, minds, and lives. May we walk daily in the fullness of His presence.

Week 33: The Power of God's Guidance and Direction

Day 224: Derekh (דֶּ֫רֶךְ)

- **Meaning:** Way, Path, Journey

- **Bible Reference:** Proverbs 3:6 – *"In all your ways (derekh) submit to Him, and He will make your paths straight."*

Message: Derekh signifies the path or journey a person takes in life. The Bible teaches that God has a specific **derekh** for each of us, a path designed for our good. However, many people stray from His way, seeking their own direction. Jesus declared, *"I am the Way (Derekh), the Truth, and the Life,"* showing that the right path is found in Him. Trusting God's **derekh** requires faith, as He often leads us step by step, not showing the entire journey at once. When we surrender to His guidance, He removes obstacles and directs our steps. Are you walking in God's **derekh**, or are you following your own way?

Reflection Questions for the Day:

1. Are you seeking God's direction for your life?

2. How can you align your path with God's **derekh**?

3. What areas of your life do you need to surrender to His way?

Day 225: Or (אוֹר)

- **Meaning:** Light, Illumination, Guidance

- **Bible Reference:** Psalm 119:105 – *"Your word is a lamp to my feet and a light (or) to my path."*

Message: Or represents light, bringing clarity and guidance to the path ahead. The world is full of darkness and confusion, but God's Word shines as a lamp, revealing the right way to go. Jesus declared, *"I am the Light (Or) of the world,"* calling us to walk in Him. Just as the sun gives physical light, God provides spiritual **or**, leading us through life's uncertainties. Without His light, we stumble, but with it, we walk securely. The more we stay in His presence, the brighter His **or** shines in our lives. Are you allowing God's **or** to guide your decisions and direction?

Reflection Questions for the Day:

1. In what ways do you seek God's light for direction?

2. Are there areas where you are walking in darkness instead of His **or**?

3. How can you let God's Word illuminate your daily life?

Day 226: Yatsah (יָצָא)

- **Meaning:** To Go Out, To Lead Forth

- **Bible Reference:** Deuteronomy 31:8 – *"The Lord Himself goes before (yatsah) you and will be with you."*

Message: Yatsah means to go out or lead forth, emphasizing God's role as our guide. He does not send us ahead blindly but goes before us, preparing the way. When the Israelites left Egypt, God **yatsah** them, leading them toward the Promised Land. In the same way, Jesus goes before His people, leading them in righteousness. Many times, we hesitate to step out in faith because we fear the unknown. But when we trust that God is **yatsah**, leading the way, we can move forward with confidence. Are you willing to follow God as He **yatsah** you into new places?

236

Reflection Questions for the Day:

1. Are you allowing God to lead you forward in life?

2. What fears are keeping you from stepping out in faith?

3. How can you trust that God is already ahead of you?

Day 227: Nachah (נָחָה)

- **Meaning:** To Lead, To Guide, To Direct

- **Bible Reference:** Psalm 23:3 – *"He guides (nachah) me along the right paths for His name's sake."*

Message: Nachah refers to God's gentle and wise guidance in our lives. The Bible describes God as a shepherd who **nachah** His sheep, leading them to safety. Unlike human leaders, God never misguides or abandons His people. Sometimes His leading is clear, but other times, we must trust Him even when we don't understand. Jesus promised that the Holy Spirit would **nachah** believers, guiding them into all truth. When we submit to God's leading, we avoid unnecessary struggles and find peace in His plans. Are you allowing God to **nachah** you, or are you resisting His direction?

Reflection Questions for the Day:

1. How do you recognize God's guidance in your life?

2. Are you willing to follow even when His direction is unclear?

3. How can you grow in your trust in God's leading?

Day 228: Paqad (פָּקַד)

237

- **Meaning:** To Visit, Oversee, Appoint

- **Bible Reference:** Jeremiah 29:10 – *"When seventy years are completed for Babylon, I will come to you and fulfill My good promise to bring you back to this place."*

Message: Paqad means to visit or oversee, signifying God's active role in directing our lives. He is not distant or unaware—He is involved in every detail. In times of hardship, we might feel abandoned, but God always **paqad** His people at the right moment. He **paqad** Sarah when she conceived Isaac, fulfilling His promise. God's timing is perfect; He **paqad** at the appointed time, bringing about His plans. When we trust in His oversight, we rest in His divine timing. Are you waiting on God's **paqad**, trusting His timing and direction?

Reflection Questions for the Day:

1. Have you experienced a time when God "visited" your situation?

2. Are you trusting in His timing, even when delays occur?

3. How can you remain faithful while waiting for God's **paqad**?

Day 229: Tsadeq (צָ‎ֿדֶ‎ק)

- **Meaning:** To Be Righteous, To Be Just, To Lead Rightly

- **Bible Reference:** Proverbs 21:3 – *"To do what is right (tsadeq) and just is more acceptable to the Lord than sacrifice."*

Message: Tsadeq means to walk in righteousness and justice, reflecting God's character. His guidance is always rooted in justice and truth, never leading us astray. When we seek God's direction, we must also seek to walk in **tsadeq**, aligning our lives with His righteousness. The Bible says that the righteous will shine like the sun in God's kingdom. Jesus is our perfect example of **tsadeq**, leading with truth and grace. Following God's guidance requires walking in righteousness and making just choices. Are you living a life of **tsadeq**, reflecting God's justice and truth?

Reflection Questions for the Day:

1. What does it mean to walk in righteousness in daily life?

2. How can you align your decisions with God's justice?

3. Are there areas in your life that need more **tsadeq**?

Day 230: Meishar (מֵ֫ישָׁ֫ר)

- **Meaning:** Uprightness, Straightness, Integrity

- **Bible Reference:** Psalm 25:8 – *"Good and upright (meishar) is the Lord; therefore He instructs sinners in His ways."*

Message: Meishar speaks of straight paths and upright living, characteristics of God's direction. His ways are not crooked or deceptive; they are clear and full of integrity. The world often presents dishonest shortcuts, but God calls us to walk in **meishar**, staying true to His truth. Jesus exemplified perfect integrity, never compromising righteousness. Walking in **meishar** brings stability and security because God honors those who live uprightly. When we follow His straight paths, we avoid many of life's pitfalls. Are you walking in **meishar**, choosing integrity over compromise?

Reflection Questions for the Day:

1. Are there any areas where you need to choose integrity over compromise?

2. How does walking in **meishar** lead to a stable life?

3. What are practical ways you can demonstrate integrity in daily decisions?

Week 33 Conclusion

This week's words reveal the many ways God directs His people. **Derekh** shows that He has a path for each of us, while **or** provides the light to walk in it. **Yatsah** reminds us that God goes before us, and **nachah** assures us of His gentle guidance. **Paqad** teaches us to trust His timing, **tsadeq** calls us to righteousness, and **meishar** emphasizes the importance of integrity. When we trust in God's guidance, we find peace, clarity, and security in His plans.

Week 34: The Power of God's Strength and Protection

Day 231: Ma'oz (מָ עוֹז)

- **Meaning:** Stronghold, Refuge, Fortress

- **Bible Reference:** Psalm 46:1 – *"God is our refuge (ma'oz) and strength, an ever-present help in trouble."*

Message: Ma'oz describes God as our stronghold and place of safety. In times of trouble, we often seek comfort in worldly solutions, but true security comes only from God. The Bible repeatedly portrays Him as a fortress, shielding His people from harm. David relied on God's **ma'oz** in battle, knowing that his strength alone was not enough. Jesus is our ultimate **ma'oz**, providing spiritual protection from sin and the enemy. No matter what challenges arise, we can trust that God's stronghold is unshakable. Are you finding refuge in God, or are you looking for security elsewhere?

Reflection Questions for the Day:

1. What does it mean for God to be your stronghold?

2. Are you placing your trust in God's protection or in temporary solutions?

3. How can you seek God's refuge in times of trouble?

Day 232: Chazaq (חָ זַ ק)

- **Meaning:** Strength, Courage, To Be Firm

- **Bible Reference:** Joshua 1:9 – *"Be strong (chazaq) and courageous. Do not be afraid; do not be discouraged, for the Lord your God will be with you wherever you go."*

Message: Chazaq represents inner strength and resilience that comes from God. Joshua was commanded to be **chazaq,**

242

not because of his own might, but because God was with him. Strength is not just physical; it is also the ability to stand firm in faith, especially in trials. Many times, fear and doubt weaken us, but God's presence gives us **chazaq** to endure. Jesus demonstrated perfect **chazaq**, facing the cross with unwavering trust in the Father. When we rely on God's power, we become unshakable. Are you drawing your strength from God, or are you relying on yourself?

Reflection Questions for the Day:

1. Where do you need God's strength in your life?

2. How can you develop greater spiritual resilience?

3. What steps can you take to trust God more in challenging situations?

Day 233: Magen (מָגֵן)

- **Meaning:** Shield, Protection, Defense

- **Bible Reference:** Psalm 3:3 – *"But You, Lord, are a shield (magen) around me, my glory, the One who lifts my head high."*

Message: Magen signifies God's protection over His people. In ancient warfare, a shield was essential for defense, blocking attacks from the enemy. The Bible frequently refers to God as our **magen**, a shield that surrounds us in times of trouble. Faith acts as a spiritual shield, deflecting the enemy's lies and doubts. Jesus is our **magen**, protecting us from sin's power and leading us in righteousness. When we trust in God's **magen**, we walk with confidence and security. Are you relying on God's protection, or are you leaving yourself vulnerable to spiritual attacks?

Reflection Questions for the Day:

1. How do you see God as your shield in your daily life?

2. Are you taking up the "shield of faith" against spiritual attacks?

3. How can you rely more on God's protection?

Day 234: Yesod (יְסוֹד)

- **Meaning:** Foundation, Stability, Support

- **Bible Reference:** Isaiah 28:16 – *"So this is what the Sovereign Lord says: 'See, I lay a stone in Zion, a tested stone, a precious cornerstone for a sure foundation (yesod); the one who relies on it will never be stricken with panic.'"*

Message: Yesod refers to a firm foundation, something stable and unmovable. Jesus is described as the **yesod**, the cornerstone upon which our faith is built. A strong foundation ensures that a structure stands firm against storms and challenges. Many people build their lives on unstable ground—wealth, success, or human wisdom—but only God's **yesod** is everlasting. When we root ourselves in Him, we gain unshakable peace and direction. The deeper our foundation in Christ, the stronger we stand. Are you building your life on the firm foundation of Jesus, or on things that will crumble?

Reflection Questions for the Day:

1. What is the foundation of your life?

2. Are you strengthening your faith in God's truth?

3. How can you ensure your foundation remains firm in Christ?

Day 235: Tzur (צוּר)

- **Meaning:** Rock, Strength, Stability

- **Bible Reference:** Psalm 18:2 – *"The Lord is my rock (tzur), my fortress and my deliverer; my God is my rock, in whom I take refuge."*

Message: Tzur represents God as our solid rock, a firm and immovable source of security. In a shifting world full of uncertainties, God remains constant. The Bible compares human wisdom to shifting sand, but those who build their lives on Christ stand firm. Jesus is our **tzur**, the cornerstone that provides stability in the storms of life. Trusting in God as our **tzur** gives us confidence that nothing can shake us. When trials come, we can stand strong, knowing our foundation is secure. Are you placing your trust in the solid rock of God, or in things that can fail?

Reflection Questions for the Day:

1. What does it mean for God to be your rock?

2. How can you build your life on His unshakable truth?

3. Are you relying on temporary foundations, or on God's stability?

Day 236: Netzach (נ_צ_ח)

- **Meaning:** Victory, Eternity, Endurance

- **Bible Reference:** 1 Samuel 15:29 – *"He who is the Glory of Israel does not lie or change His mind; for He is not a human being, that He should change His mind."*

Message: Netzach means both victory and eternity, emphasizing God's never-ending power and triumph. In battle, God's people trusted Him for **netzach**, knowing He never fails. Jesus' resurrection is the greatest example of **netzach**, proving His victory over sin and death. As believers, we share in His victory, called to walk in triumph over fear, sin, and doubt. **Netzach** is not just about winning battles—it is about enduring in faith, knowing that ultimate victory belongs to God. Even in struggles, His **netzach** sustains us, assuring us that He is in control. Are you living in the victory of Christ, or are you allowing defeat to define you?

Reflection Questions for the Day:

1. How does Jesus' victory influence your daily life?

2. Are you walking in faith, knowing that victory belongs to God?

3. What struggles are you facing where you need to claim God's **netzach**?

Day 237: Selah (סֶ֫לָה)

- **Meaning:** Pause, Reflect, Rest in God

- **Bible Reference:** Psalm 46:10 – *"Be still, and know that I am God."*

Message: Selah is a word found throughout the Psalms, calling for a pause and reflection on God's greatness. In the rush of life, we often forget to stop and acknowledge God's presence. True strength comes not from constant striving but from resting in God's sovereignty. Jesus frequently withdrew to be alone with the Father, demonstrating the importance of **Selah** moments. When we take time to meditate on God's power, we gain renewed strength and perspective. Pausing in God's presence allows us to move forward with greater clarity. Are you making space for **Selah**, allowing God to renew and strengthen you?

Reflection Questions for the Day:

1. Do you take time to pause and reflect on God's presence?

2. How does rest in God strengthen you spiritually?

3. What can you do to incorporate **Selah** into your daily routine?

Week 34 Conclusion

This week's words remind us that God is our fortress and protector. **Ma'oz** declares Him as our refuge, while **chazaq** empowers us with strength. **Magen** shields us, and **yesod** provides a firm foundation. **Tzur** confirms that He is our unshakable rock, and **netzach** assures us of His eternal victory. **Selah** invites us to rest in His power. When we rely on God's strength, we find security, endurance, and lasting peace.

Week 35: The Power of God's Provision and Blessings

Day 238: Yireh (יִ ר אָ ה)

- **Meaning:** Will Provide, See to It

- **Bible Reference:** Genesis 22:14 – *"So Abraham called that place 'The Lord Will Provide (Yireh).' And to this day it is said, 'On the mountain of the Lord it will be provided.'"*

Message: **Yireh** is the name Abraham used to describe God after He provided a ram in place of Isaac. This name, *Yahweh-Yireh*, means that God sees our needs and provides for them at the right time. Just as He provided for Abraham, God still meets the needs of His children today. His provision is not always what we expect, but it is always what we truly need. Jesus is our ultimate **Yireh**, as He provided salvation through His sacrifice. Trusting in God's **Yireh** means surrendering our worries and believing that He will take care of us. Are you trusting in God's provision, or are you trying to meet your needs on your own?

Reflection Questions for the Day:

1. How has God provided for you in the past?

2. Do you fully trust that He will continue to provide?

3. What areas of your life do you need to surrender to God's **Yireh**?

Day 239: Lechem (לְ ח ֶם)

- **Meaning:** Bread, Sustenance, Daily Provision

- **Bible Reference:** John 6:35 – *"Then Jesus declared, 'I am the Bread (Lechem) of life. Whoever comes to Me will never go hungry, and whoever believes in Me will never be thirsty.'"*

249

Message: Lechem represents both physical food and spiritual nourishment. In the Old Testament, God provided **lechem** (manna) for Israel in the wilderness, teaching them to depend on Him daily. Jesus referred to Himself as the **Lechem** of Life, offering eternal satisfaction that goes beyond physical needs. Just as we need food to survive, we need Jesus to sustain our souls. When we rely on Him, we are spiritually nourished and strengthened. Seeking God's **lechem** daily means coming to Him in prayer, studying His Word, and trusting in His sufficiency. Are you feeding your soul with the **Lechem** of Life, or are you seeking fulfillment elsewhere?

Reflection Questions for the Day:

1. How do you seek daily spiritual nourishment?

2. Are you relying on Jesus as your **Lechem**, or are you looking to other sources for satisfaction?

3. What changes can you make to hunger more for God's Word?

Day 240: Revayah (רְ,וָ,יָ,ה)

- **Meaning:** Overflow, Abundance, Fullness

- **Bible Reference:** Psalm 23:5 – *"You anoint my head with oil; my cup overflows (revayah)."*

Message: Revayah describes the abundant blessings of God, where He provides not just enough but more than enough. David recognized God's overflowing provision, not only in physical needs but in peace, joy, and love. Jesus came to give us life in abundance, not a life of scarcity and lack. God's **revayah** allows us to bless others, as His overflow in our lives spills into the lives of those around us. However, true

250

abundance is not measured by material wealth but by a heart full of gratitude and generosity. The more we trust in God's **revayah**, the more we experience His goodness. Are you living in the overflow of God's blessings, or are you limiting His work in your life?

Reflection Questions for the Day:

1. What areas of your life reflect God's overflow?

2. Are you sharing God's abundance with others, or holding onto it selfishly?

3. How can you cultivate a heart of gratitude for God's **revayah**?

Day 241: Matar (מָטָר)

- **Meaning:** Rain, Heavenly Blessings

- **Bible Reference:** Deuteronomy 11:14 – *"Then I will send rain (matar) on your land in its season, both autumn and spring rains, so that you may gather in your grain, new wine, and olive oil."*

Message: Matar represents God's blessing and provision, often symbolized by rain that nourishes the land. Without **matar**, crops would wither, and people would suffer famine. Just as physical rain is necessary for growth, God's spiritual **matar** refreshes and renews us. The Bible describes God's Word and His Spirit as **matar**, reviving weary souls. Sometimes, we go through dry seasons, but God promises to send His **matar** at the right time. Trusting in God's provision means believing He will bring the rain when it is needed most. Are you waiting for God's **matar**, trusting that He will send His blessings in due season?

Reflection Questions for the Day:

1. What areas of your life feel spiritually dry?

2. How can you prepare your heart to receive God's **matar**?

3. Do you trust that God will provide in His perfect timing?

Day 242: Nachalah (נַ_חֲ_לָ_ה)

- **Meaning:** Inheritance, Heritage, Possession

- **Bible Reference:** Deuteronomy 26:1 – *"When you have entered the land the Lord your God is giving you as an inheritance (nachalah) and have taken possession of it and settled in it."*

Message: Nachalah refers to an inheritance, something received not because of effort but as a gift. Israel's Promised Land was their **nachalah**, a blessing from God meant to be treasured and stewarded well. As believers, we also have a spiritual **nachalah**—the inheritance of eternal life and the riches of God's kingdom. Many Christians live as spiritual beggars when they have a divine inheritance waiting for them. Jesus secured our **nachalah**, giving us access to God's promises. Are you embracing your **nachalah**, walking in the fullness of God's blessings?

Reflection Questions for the Day:

1. What does it mean for you to have a spiritual inheritance?

2. Are you living in the fullness of what God has provided?

3. How can you steward God's blessings wisely?

Day 243: Shalom (שָׁלוֹם)

- **Meaning:** Peace, Wholeness, Complete Well-being

- **Bible Reference:** Numbers 6:24-26 – *"The Lord bless you and keep you; the Lord make His face shine on you and be gracious to you; the Lord turn His face toward you and give you peace (shalom)."*

Message: Shalom is more than just peace—it is complete well-being, wholeness, and the blessing of God's presence. God's **shalom** brings rest, healing, and restoration, filling every area of our lives. The world offers temporary peace, but true **shalom** comes only from God. Jesus is the Prince of **Shalom**, and through Him, we receive peace with God and peace within ourselves. Living in **shalom** means trusting in God's sovereignty, even in difficult circumstances. When we abide in Christ, we experience His deep and lasting **shalom**. Are you embracing God's **shalom**, or are you allowing worry and fear to steal your peace?

Reflection Questions for the Day:

1. How do you define true peace in your life?

2. Are you resting in God's **shalom**, or are you overwhelmed by stress?

3. What steps can you take to cultivate a heart of **shalom**?

Week 35 Conclusion

This week's words remind us that God is our provider and source of every blessing. **Yireh** assures us that He will meet our needs, while **lechem** reminds us that Jesus is our spiritual nourishment. **Revayah** speaks of God's overflow, and **matar** symbolizes His abundant blessings. **Nachalah** confirms that we have an inheritance in Him, and **shalom** brings peace to our hearts. Trusting in God's provision leads to a life of faith, gratitude, and contentment.

Week 36: The Power of God's Love and Compassion

Day 244: Ahavah (אֲהַבָה)

- **Meaning:** Love, Devotion, Deep Affection

- **Bible Reference:** Deuteronomy 6:5 – *"Love (ahavah) the Lord your God with all your heart and with all your soul and with all your strength."*

Message: Ahavah is a deep, enduring love that goes beyond emotion—it is an act of will and devotion. The Bible describes God's **ahavah** as unconditional, a love that is not based on our performance but on His character. Jesus demonstrated perfect **ahavah** by laying down His life for us, showing that true love is sacrificial. Love is not just a feeling but a choice to serve, forgive, and honor others. God calls us to love Him with all our hearts and to extend His **ahavah** to those around us. When we live in His love, we reflect His nature. Are you walking in **ahavah**, loving God and others as He commands?

Reflection Questions for the Day:

1. How do you demonstrate love for God in your daily life?

2. Are you extending God's **ahavah** to others, even when it's difficult?

3. What can you do to deepen your love for God and people?

Day 245: Chesed (חֶסֶד)

- **Meaning:** Loving-kindness, Covenant Mercy, Unfailing Love

- **Bible Reference:** Lamentations 3:22 – *"Because of the Lord's great love (chesed) we are not consumed, for His compassions never fail."*

Message: Chesed is a loyal, steadfast love that is rooted in covenant commitment. Unlike human love, which can change based on circumstances, God's **chesed** is enduring and unbreakable. Throughout the Bible, God's **chesed** is displayed in His patience and faithfulness toward His people. Even when Israel rebelled, God's **chesed** remained, calling them back to Him. Jesus embodied **chesed**, showing kindness and mercy to sinners. As recipients of God's **chesed**, we are called to extend the same loving-kindness to others. Are you embracing and sharing the **chesed** of God in your life?

Reflection Questions for the Day:

1. How have you experienced God's **chesed** in your life?

2. Are you showing steadfast love and kindness to others?

3. How can you cultivate a heart that reflects God's **chesed**?

Day 246: Rachamim (ר_ח_מ_ים)

- **Meaning:** Compassion, Tender Mercy, Deep Affection

- **Bible Reference:** Psalm 103:13 – *"As a father has compassion (rachamim) on his children, so the Lord has compassion on those who fear Him."*

Message: Rachamim comes from the root word *rechem*, meaning "womb," signifying a deep, nurturing love like that of a mother for her child. God's **rachamim** is not distant or indifferent—it is personal, tender, and full of mercy. The Bible is filled with examples of God's **rachamim**, from rescuing Israel to healing the sick through Jesus. Jesus had deep **rachamim** for the lost and broken, showing mercy to those who least deserved it. As His followers, we are called to embody His **rachamim**, showing compassion to others. Are you living with a heart full of **rachamim**, extending God's mercy to those around you?

Reflection Questions for the Day:

1. When have you experienced God's compassion in your life?

2. How can you show more **rachamim** to those in need?

3. Are you allowing God's tender mercy to shape your interactions with others?

Day 247: Dodi (דּוֹד י)

- **Meaning:** My Beloved, Deep Personal Love

- **Bible Reference:** Song of Solomon 2:16 – *"My beloved (dodi) is mine and I am his; he browses among the lilies."*

Message: Dodi expresses a deep, intimate love, often used in a romantic sense but also reflecting God's love for His people. The Song of Solomon portrays the love between a bride and groom as a symbol of God's love for His church. The Bible frequently describes God as our **dodi**, drawing us into a personal, affectionate relationship. Jesus refers to His followers as His bride, highlighting the closeness and devotion He desires from us. God's **dodi** love is not distant but deeply relational. Are you embracing God's intimate love, or are you keeping Him at a distance?

Reflection Questions for the Day:

1. How does knowing God loves you deeply impact your faith?

2. Are you allowing yourself to experience God's **dodi** love personally?

3. What steps can you take to grow closer in your relationship with Him?

Day 248: Chanan (חָ‎נַ‎ן)

- **Meaning:** To Be Gracious, Show Favor

- **Bible Reference:** Numbers 6:25 – *"The Lord make His face shine on you and be gracious (chanan) to you."*

Message: Chanan is God's favor, His unearned grace that He pours out abundantly. We see His **chanan** throughout Scripture, from His provision for Israel to His ultimate gift of salvation through Jesus. Grace is not something we earn—it is freely given by God's love. Jesus embodied **chanan**, offering forgiveness to sinners and favor to the undeserving. As recipients of God's **chanan**, we are called to extend grace to others, forgiving as He has forgiven us. Living in God's grace means trusting His goodness and sharing it with those around us. Are you embracing God's **chanan**, and are you showing grace to others?

Reflection Questions for the Day:

1. How have you experienced God's grace in your life?

2. Are you extending grace and forgiveness to others?

3. What does it mean to live daily in God's **chanan**?

Day 249: Eleos (Έλεος)

- **Meaning:** Mercy, Loving-Kindness, Divine Favor

- **Bible Reference:** Luke 1:50 – *"His mercy (eleos) extends to those who fear Him, from generation to generation."*

Message: Eleos is the Greek equivalent of **chesed**, describing God's mercy and kindness that extends to generations. Mary's song of praise in Luke 1 declares that God's **eleos** is unending, reaching those who trust in Him. Jesus consistently showed **eleos**, healing the sick, forgiving sinners, and teaching about God's mercy. When we receive God's **eleos**, we are freed from condemnation and given new life. Mercy is not just for us to enjoy—it is for us to share with the world. Are you reflecting God's **eleos**, showing mercy and kindness to others?

Reflection Questions for the Day:

1. What does God's mercy mean to you personally?

2. Are you quick to show **eleos** to others, or do you withhold forgiveness?

3. How can you be a vessel of God's mercy in your daily life?

Day 250: Dod (דּוֹד)

- **Meaning:** Love, Friendship, Beloved Companion

- **Bible Reference:** Proverbs 17:17 – *"A friend (dod) loves at all times, and a brother is born for a time of adversity."*

Message: Dod signifies love in the context of deep friendship and companionship. The Bible teaches that love is not just romantic—it is about loyalty, trust, and standing by each other in difficult times. God calls us into loving relationships, first with Him and then with others. Jesus called His disciples friends, showing that love is about deep, lasting commitment. True **dod** love is selfless, seeking the good of others. When we cultivate **dod** love, we build strong relationships that reflect God's heart. Are you practicing **dod** love in your friendships, reflecting God's faithfulness?

Reflection Questions for the Day:

1. How can you cultivate godly friendships in your life?

2. Are you being a faithful, loving friend to others?

3. How does Jesus' example of friendship inspire you?

Week 36 Conclusion

This week's words reveal the depth of God's love. **Ahavah** calls us to love God and others, while **chesed** and **rachamim** remind us of His steadfast mercy. **Dodi** and **dod** show the intimate and faithful aspects of love, and **chanan** and **eleos** highlight God's grace and mercy. When we live in His love, we reflect His heart to the world. May we walk in His unfailing love and share it with others.

Week 37: The Power of God's Justice and Righteousness

Day 251: Mishpat (מִ‎שְׁ‎פָּ‎ט)

- **Meaning:** Justice, Judgment, Righteous Law

- **Bible Reference:** Micah 6:8 – *"He has shown you, O mortal, what is good. And what does the Lord require of you? To act justly (mishpat) and to love mercy and to walk humbly with your God."*

Message: Mishpat represents God's justice—His righteous way of setting things right. Throughout Scripture, God commands His people to practice **mishpat**, treating others fairly and upholding truth. Unlike human justice, which can be biased or flawed, God's **mishpat** is perfect, bringing both fairness and mercy. Jesus exemplified **mishpat**, confronting injustice while offering redemption. As followers of Christ, we are called to seek justice in our own lives, standing against oppression and advocating for truth. When we align ourselves with God's **mishpat**, we reflect His kingdom on earth. Are you committed to living out God's justice in your daily life?

Reflection Questions for the Day:

1. How do you personally seek justice in your life?

2. Are there areas where you need to stand up for God's **mishpat**?

3. How can you balance justice with mercy in your relationships?

Day 252: Tzedek (צֶ‎דֶ‎ק)

- **Meaning:** Righteousness, Uprightness, Moral Integrity

- **Bible Reference:** Psalm 89:14 – *"Righteousness (tzedek) and justice are the foundation of Your throne; love and faithfulness go before You."*

Message: Tzedek refers to righteousness, a life lived in moral integrity and obedience to God. It is not just about avoiding sin but actively pursuing what is good and just. God's throne is established on **tzedek**, meaning that His rule is always right and true. Jesus, the Righteous One, demonstrated perfect **tzedek**, living blamelessly before God and man. We are called to seek **tzedek**, allowing His righteousness to transform our character and actions. Living righteously brings peace and favor, aligning our hearts with God's holiness. Are you seeking to walk in **tzedek**, displaying God's righteousness in all you do?

Reflection Questions for the Day:

1. What does it mean to live righteously before God?

2. Are there areas in your life where you need to grow in **tzedek**?

3. How can you reflect God's righteousness in your daily decisions?

Day 253: Yosher (יָשֵׁר)

- **Meaning:** Uprightness, Honesty, Integrity

- **Bible Reference:** Proverbs 11:3 – *"The integrity (yosher) of the upright guides them, but the unfaithful are destroyed by their duplicity."*

Message: Yosher is about living with honesty and moral integrity, remaining upright even when no one is watching. The Bible teaches that **yosher** leads to blessings and stability, while deception leads to destruction. Jesus was the ultimate example of **yosher**, never compromising truth for personal gain. The world often tempts us to cut corners or justify small compromises, but true righteousness requires unwavering integrity. People trust those who live in **yosher**, and God honors those who walk in truth. Integrity is not just about avoiding wrongdoing but consistently choosing what is right. Are you walking in **yosher**, maintaining honesty in all areas of your life?

Reflection Questions for the Day:

1. How does integrity influence your decisions and relationships?

2. Are there areas where you struggle to be completely honest?

3. How can you strengthen your commitment to **yosher** in daily life?

Day 254: Emet (אֱמֶת)

- **Meaning:** Truth, Faithfulness, Reliability

- **Bible Reference:** Psalm 119:160 – *"All Your words are true (emet); all Your righteous laws are eternal."*

Message: **Emet** means truth, both in the sense of what is factual and what is faithful. God's Word is **emet**, unchanging and reliable through every season. Jesus declared, *"I am the Way, the Truth (Emet), and the Life,"* showing that truth is not just an idea but a person. Living in **emet** means embracing truth in all things—our beliefs, words, and actions. The enemy operates in lies, but God calls us to walk in His truth. When we hold to **emet**, we build our lives on a firm foundation. Are you living in the truth of God's **emet**, or are you influenced by the world's falsehoods?

Reflection Questions for the Day:

1. How do you determine what is true in your life?

2. Are you standing firm on God's **emet**, or are you swayed by deception?

3. How can you walk in greater truth and faithfulness?

Day 255: Dan (דָּן)

- **Meaning:** To Judge, To Bring Justice

- **Bible Reference:** Genesis 18:25 – *"Will not the Judge (dan) of all the earth do right?"*

Message: Dan means to judge or bring justice, emphasizing God's role as the ultimate judge. Unlike human judges, who can be biased or make mistakes, God's judgments are always just and perfect. Throughout Scripture, God executes justice, punishing wickedness while upholding righteousness. Jesus, though full of grace, also spoke about judgment, reminding us that God will hold all people accountable. While we are not called to condemn, we are called to discern rightly and uphold God's justice in our actions. Trusting in God's **dan** means believing that He will right every wrong in His perfect timing. Are you trusting in God's justice, or are you trying to take judgment into your own hands?

Reflection Questions for the Day:

1. How do you balance justice with grace in your life?

2. Are you trusting God to bring justice where it is needed?

3. How can you uphold godly justice in your relationships and community?

Day 256: Tsedeqah (צ,ד,ק,ה)

- **Meaning:** Righteousness Expressed Through Generosity and Justice

- **Bible Reference:** Proverbs 21:21 – *"Whoever pursues righteousness (tsedeqah) and love finds life, prosperity, and honor."*

Message: **Tsedeqah** combines righteousness with acts of charity and justice. In biblical times, righteousness was not just about personal morality but about caring for the poor and helping the vulnerable. Jesus emphasized **tsedeqah**, teaching that true faith is demonstrated in love and generosity. The early church practiced this by sharing resources so that no one was in need. When we live in **tsedeqah**, we reflect God's heart for justice and mercy. Generosity is not just about money—it is about time, compassion, and standing for truth. Are you practicing **tsedeqah**, using what you have to bless and uplift others?

Reflection Questions for the Day:

1. How does righteousness relate to generosity in your life?

2. Are you actively helping those in need as part of your faith?

3. What steps can you take to grow in **tsedeqah**?

Day 257: Shafat (שׁ,פ,ט)

- **Meaning:** To Govern, To Bring Justice, To Rule Rightly

- **Bible Reference:** Isaiah 1:17 – *"Learn to do right; seek justice (shafat). Defend the oppressed. Take up the cause of the fatherless; plead the case of the widow."*

Message: Shafat refers to the act of governing or judging rightly. Throughout the Bible, God raised up judges (shoftim) to lead Israel and bring justice to the people. However, human rulers often failed, showing that true **shafat** comes only from God. Jesus is the ultimate righteous Judge, who will one day establish His kingdom in perfect justice. As His followers, we are called to seek justice, not through worldly power, but through truth, love, and righteousness. When we practice **shafat**, we align ourselves with God's kingdom values. Are you standing for godly justice in the way you live and treat others?

Reflection Questions for the Day:

1. How does God's justice influence your worldview?

2. Are you standing for righteousness and truth in your community?

3. What can you do to live out God's call to justice?

Week 37 Conclusion

This week's words reveal the importance of living in God's justice. **Mishpat** and **tzedek** remind us to uphold righteousness, while **yosher** and **emet** call us to integrity and truth. **Dan** and **shafat** reveal God's role as the ultimate judge, and **tsedeqah** emphasizes that righteousness includes generosity and justice. When we align ourselves with God's justice, we reflect His character and bring His kingdom to earth.

Week 38: The Power of God's Deliverance and Redemption

Day 258: Ga'al (גָּאַל)

- **Meaning:** To Redeem, To Buy Back, To Deliver

- **Bible Reference:** Isaiah 43:1 – *"Do not fear, for I have redeemed (ga'al) you; I have summoned you by name; you are mine."*

Message: Ga'al represents God's act of redemption, buying back His people from bondage. In the Old Testament, a **go'el** (redeemer) was responsible for restoring a family member's lost property or freedom. Boaz acted as Ruth's **go'el**, symbolizing Christ's ultimate redemption of humanity. Jesus, through His sacrifice, became our **go'el**, redeeming us from sin and giving us new life. Redemption is not just about being saved from something but being restored for a purpose. Because of God's **ga'al**, we belong to Him, freed from guilt and shame. Are you living in the freedom of God's redemption, or are you still bound by the past?

Reflection Questions for the Day:

1. What does redemption mean in your personal faith journey?

2. Are you fully embracing the freedom that comes with being redeemed?

3. How can you share the message of God's **ga'al** with others?

Day 259: Pidyon (פִּדְיוֹן)

- **Meaning:** Ransom, Atonement, Redemption Price

- **Bible Reference:** Psalm 49:7-8 – *"No one can redeem (pidyon) the life of another or give to God a ransom for them—the ransom for a life is costly."*

Message: Pidyon refers to the price of redemption, the ransom required to free someone from captivity. In biblical times, the firstborn sons were consecrated to God and could be "redeemed" through **pidyon**. Spiritually, no amount of wealth or good works could serve as **pidyon** for sin—only Jesus' sacrifice was enough. His death was the ultimate **pidyon**, paying the debt we could never repay. Because of His ransom, we are no longer slaves to sin but children of God. Understanding the cost of our redemption should lead us to gratitude and devotion. Are you living in the reality that Jesus paid the full **pidyon** for your life?

Reflection Questions for the Day:

1. What does it mean that Jesus paid the ransom for you?

2. Are you living as someone who has been fully redeemed?

3. How can gratitude for your **pidyon** lead you to a deeper relationship with Christ?

Day 260: Yeshuah (יְשׁוּעָה)

- **Meaning:** Salvation, Deliverance, Rescue

- **Bible Reference:** Exodus 15:2 – *"The Lord is my strength and my defense; He has become my salvation (yeshuah)."*

Message: Yeshuah means salvation and deliverance, and it is closely connected to the name of Jesus (Yeshua), who is our Savior. Throughout the Old Testament, God provided **yeshuah** for His people, rescuing them from Egypt, enemies, and sin. Jesus fulfilled this ultimate salvation, delivering us from spiritual death into eternal life. **Yeshuah** is not just about the afterlife; it is about experiencing freedom and

271

transformation now. When we trust in God's **yeshuah**, we find peace and security, knowing He fights for us. The question is not whether salvation is available but whether we are embracing it fully. Are you living in the joy of God's **yeshuah**, or are you still trying to save yourself?

Reflection Questions for the Day:

1. How does salvation impact your daily life?

2. Are you trusting in God's **yeshuah**, or are you relying on your own strength?

3. How can you share the message of **yeshuah** with others?

Day 261: Natzal (נָ_צַ_ל)

- **Meaning:** To Deliver, To Snatch Away, To Rescue

- **Bible Reference:** Psalm 34:17 – *"The righteous cry out, and the Lord hears them; He delivers (natzal) them from all their troubles."*

Message: Natzal describes God's power to rescue and deliver His people from danger. In Scripture, He **natzal** Noah from the flood, Lot from Sodom, and Israel from Pharaoh. God is not distant; He actively steps in to save His people when they cry out to Him. However, His deliverance is not always immediate or in the way we expect. Sometimes, deliverance means walking through trials with His presence instead of avoiding them altogether. Trusting in God's **natzal** means believing He is working even when we don't see it. Are you trusting in His power to rescue you from your struggles?

Reflection Questions for the Day:

1. When has God delivered you from a difficult situation?

2. Are you waiting for deliverance in any area of your life?

3. How can you grow in trusting God's plan for rescue?

Day 262: Chatta'ah (חַ ְטָ ָאה)

- **Meaning:** Sin Offering, Atonement, Purification

- **Bible Reference:** Leviticus 4:3 – *"If the anointed priest sins, bringing guilt on the people, he must bring to the Lord a young bull without defect as a sin offering (chatta'ah) for the sin he has committed."*

Message: Chatta'ah refers to a sin offering, a sacrifice made to atone for wrongdoing. In the Old Testament, sacrifices were required to cover sins, pointing to the ultimate sacrifice of Jesus. He became the perfect **chatta'ah**, taking our sins upon Himself so that we could be made clean. Unlike animal sacrifices, which had to be repeated, Jesus' atonement was once and for all. His blood washes away our sins, giving us access to God's presence. Living in this truth means repenting and receiving His grace daily. Are you walking in the freedom of Christ's perfect **chatta'ah**, or are you still carrying guilt?

Reflection Questions for the Day:

1. How does Jesus' sacrifice change the way you view sin?

2. Are you still trying to "earn" forgiveness, or are you resting in His atonement?

3. How can you live in the freedom of God's grace?

Day 263: Kaphar (כ.פ.ר)

- **Meaning:** To Cover, To Make Atonement, To Reconcile

- **Bible Reference:** Leviticus 17:11 – *"For the life of a creature is in the blood, and I have given it to you to make atonement (kaphar) for yourselves on the altar."*

Message: Kaphar means to cover or make atonement, symbolizing God's mercy in forgiving sin. The Day of Atonement (Yom Kippur) was a time when the High Priest would sprinkle blood on the mercy seat to **kaphar** the sins of Israel. Jesus' sacrifice fulfilled this permanently, covering our sins and reconciling us to God. Because of His **kaphar**, we are no longer separated from Him—we have full access to His presence. This covering is not temporary but eternal, freeing us to live in grace. Are you living in the reality of God's **kaphar**, fully embracing His atonement for you?

Reflection Questions for the Day:

1. What does it mean to be fully covered by God's grace?

2. Are you living in guilt, or in the freedom of God's atonement?

3. How can you reflect God's atoning love to others?

Week 38 Conclusion

This week's words reveal the depth of God's redemption. **Ga'al** and **pidyon** show that we were bought at a price, while **yeshuah** and **natzal** remind us that God is our rescuer. **Chatta'ah** and **kaphar** highlight Jesus' perfect sacrifice, which cleanses and restores us. God's redemption is not just about escaping judgment—it is about being restored for a purpose. When we accept His salvation fully, we walk in freedom, gratitude, and love.

Week 39: The Power of God's Covenant and Promises

Day 264: Brit (בְּ רִ ית)

- **Meaning:** Covenant, Agreement, Divine Promise

- **Bible Reference:** Genesis 17:7 – *"I will establish My covenant (brit) as an everlasting covenant between Me and you and your descendants after you for the generations to come, to be your God and the God of your descendants after you."*

Message: **Brit** is a sacred agreement, often initiated by God to express His unbreakable promises. In the Old Testament, God made covenants with Noah, Abraham, Moses, and David, each reinforcing His faithfulness. The ultimate **brit** was fulfilled through Jesus, whose sacrifice established the New Covenant of grace. Unlike human contracts that depend on both parties, God's **brit** is based on His unwavering character. Through this covenant, we are invited into a relationship of trust, obedience, and blessing. Knowing we are part of God's **brit** brings security and assurance of His unchanging love. Are you living in the confidence of God's covenant, trusting in His promises?

Reflection Questions for the Day:

1. What does God's covenant mean for your relationship with Him?

2. Are you embracing the New Covenant through Jesus fully?

3. How does God's faithfulness in His **brit** impact your daily life?

Day 265: Zakar (זָ כַ ר)

- **Meaning:** To Remember, To Keep in Mind, To Be Mindful

- **Bible Reference:** Deuteronomy 8:18 – *"But remember (zakar) the Lord your God, for it is He who gives you the ability to produce wealth."*

Message: Zakar is the act of intentionally remembering God's faithfulness, His commands, and His covenant. Forgetting leads to doubt and disobedience, while remembering strengthens faith and obedience. The Israelites were commanded to **zakar** God's laws and His deliverance from Egypt, ensuring they remained faithful. Jesus instituted the Lord's Supper as a way to **zakar** His sacrifice, keeping our hearts aligned with Him. When we make time to **zakar** God's goodness, we are less likely to stray. Gratitude is deeply connected to remembering, as we acknowledge all He has done. Are you making an effort to **zakar** God's promises, or are you allowing distractions to cloud your faith?

Reflection Questions for the Day:

1. How has God been faithful to you in the past?

2. What practices can help you **zakar** God's promises daily?

3. How does remembering God's faithfulness strengthen your trust in Him?

Day 266: Emunah (אֱמוּנָה)

- **Meaning:** Faith, Trust, Steadfastness

- **Bible Reference:** Habakkuk 2:4 – *"The righteous will live by his faith (emunah)."*

Message: Emunah is not just intellectual belief; it is a steadfast trust in God's character and promises. Abraham exemplified **emunah** when he believed God's promise despite his old age. Faith requires perseverance, especially when circumstances seem uncertain. Jesus called His followers to have faith that moves mountains, showing that **emunah** brings divine power into our lives. The Bible warns that without faith, it is impossible to please God. Trusting in God's **emunah** means resting in His plans, even when we don't see the full picture. Are you walking in **emunah**, trusting God completely, or are you relying on your own understanding?

Reflection Questions for the Day:

1. What challenges have tested your faith recently?

2. How can you strengthen your **emunah** in God's promises?

3. Are you trusting God even when answers are delayed?

Day 267: Ne'eman (נֶאֱמָן)

- **Meaning:** Faithful, Loyal, Trustworthy

- **Bible Reference:** 2 Timothy 2:13 – *"If we are faithless, He remains faithful (ne'eman), for He cannot disown Himself."*

Message: Ne'eman describes God's absolute faithfulness, showing that He is always trustworthy. Even when we fail, God remains **ne'eman**, keeping His promises and His love unwavering. Throughout Scripture, we see His faithfulness in fulfilling His covenants, providing for His people, and sending the Messiah. Jesus embodied **ne'eman**, staying faithful to the Father's will, even unto death. As followers of

Christ, we are called to be **ne'eman** in our commitment to Him and in our relationships with others. The world may change, but God's **ne'eman** is eternal. Are you reflecting God's faithfulness in your own life?

Reflection Questions for the Day:

1. How have you experienced God's faithfulness personally?

2. Are you demonstrating **ne'eman** in your walk with God and others?

3. How can you strengthen your commitment to faithfulness in all areas of life?

Day 268: Qavah (קָוָה)

- **Meaning:** To Wait, To Hope, To Trust Expectantly

- **Bible Reference:** Isaiah 40:31 – *"But those who wait (qavah) on the Lord will renew their strength."*

Message: Qavah is not passive waiting; it is active hope and expectation in God's timing and promises. The Bible is filled with people who had to **qavah**—Abraham waited for Isaac, Joseph waited for his purpose, and David waited to become king. God's timing is perfect, though it often requires patience and endurance. **Qavah** brings renewed strength, teaching us dependence on God rather than our own abilities. When we trust in God's **qavah**, we find peace in the waiting, knowing He is at work. The question is not whether God will act, but whether we are willing to trust Him while we wait. Are you practicing **qavah**, waiting on God with expectant faith?

Reflection Questions for the Day:

1. What are you waiting on God for right now?

2. How can you wait with faith and not frustration?

3. Are you trusting that God's timing is perfect?

Day 269: Dabar (דָּבָר)

- **Meaning:** Word, Promise, Matter, Decree

- **Bible Reference:** Isaiah 55:11 – *"So is My word (dabar) that goes out from My mouth: It will not return to Me empty."*

Message: Dabar signifies God's spoken word, His promises, and the certainty of His decrees. When God speaks, His **dabar** carries power, creating and sustaining the universe. His promises are not empty words but unshakable truths. Jesus, as the living Word, is the fulfillment of God's **dabar**, bringing life and salvation. We are called to stand firm on His **dabar**, believing in His promises even when circumstances seem contrary. His Word never fails, and His truth endures forever. Are you aligning your life with God's **dabar**, trusting in His promises?

Reflection Questions for the Day:

1. How do you see God's **dabar** active in your life?

2. Are you speaking and declaring His promises over your situations?

3. How can you deepen your trust in God's Word?

Week 39 Conclusion

This week's words emphasize God's faithfulness in keeping His promises. **Brit** establishes His covenant, while **zakar** reminds us to remember His faithfulness. **Emunah** and

281

ne'eman show the importance of trusting in His reliability. **Qavah** teaches us to wait expectantly, and **dabar** confirms that His Word never fails. When we embrace God's promises, we live in confidence and peace, knowing He is always true to His Word. His covenant is everlasting, and His faithfulness endures through all generations.

Week 40: The Power of God's Wisdom and Understanding

Day 270: Sekhel (שֵׂ כֶ ל)

- **Meaning:** Intelligence, Insight, Prudence, Common Sense

- **Bible Reference:** Proverbs 19:11 – *"A person's wisdom (sekhel) yields patience; it is to one's glory to overlook an offense."*

Message: Sekhel represents practical wisdom—the ability to apply knowledge in everyday situations. The Bible teaches that wisdom is more valuable than gold, and those who seek it will find success. God calls us to develop **sekhel**, using discernment in our decisions rather than acting impulsively. Jesus displayed perfect **sekhel**, knowing when to speak, when to remain silent, and how to answer His opponents with wisdom. Many people gain knowledge but lack **sekhel**, making foolish choices despite knowing the truth. True wisdom comes from God, and He grants it to those who ask. Are you seeking God's **sekhel** in your daily decisions, or are you relying on your own understanding?

Reflection Questions for the Day:

1. How do you apply wisdom in your daily life?

2. Are you seeking God's guidance before making important decisions?

3. How can you grow in **sekhel** and discernment?

Day 271: Binah (בִּ ינָ ה)

- **Meaning:** Discernment, Understanding, Insight

- **Bible Reference:** Proverbs 4:7 – *"The beginning of wisdom is this: Get wisdom. Though it cost all you have, get understanding (binah)."*

Message: Binah is the ability to see beyond the surface, understanding the deeper meaning of things. Many people acquire knowledge but lack **binah**, failing to grasp how truth applies to their lives. The Bible teaches that **binah** is a gift from God, helping us navigate life's complexities. Jesus demonstrated **binah** by perceiving people's thoughts and motivations, responding with wisdom beyond human ability. When we seek **binah**, we develop spiritual discernment, recognizing truth from deception. God desires for His people to have **binah**, so they are not easily led astray. Are you asking God for **binah**, or are you relying only on human reasoning?

Reflection Questions for the Day:

1. How do you seek deeper understanding in your faith?

2. Are you developing discernment to recognize truth from deception?

3. What practical steps can you take to grow in **binah**?

Day 272: Da'at (דַּ_עַ_ת)

- **Meaning:** Knowledge, Awareness, Perception

- **Bible Reference:** Proverbs 2:6 – *"For the Lord gives wisdom; from His mouth come knowledge (da'at) and understanding."*

Message: Da'at represents knowledge, but in the biblical sense, it is more than information—it is relational and spiritual understanding. Adam and Eve were warned not to eat from the Tree of the Knowledge (**da'at**) of Good and Evil, showing that **da'at** can be used righteously or destructively. True **da'at** comes from knowing God personally, not just acquiring facts about Him. Jesus invited people to grow in **da'at** by following Him, rather than merely memorizing religious laws. In a world filled with endless information, we need God's **da'at** to know what is true and worthwhile. Are you pursuing **da'at** that leads to wisdom, or are you just collecting knowledge without application?

Reflection Questions for the Day:

1. How do you differentiate between worldly knowledge and godly **da'at**?

2. Are you seeking a deeper relationship with God to grow in true knowledge?

3. How can you apply what you learn in a way that honors God?

Day 273: Ormah (עָרְמָ□ה)

- **Meaning:** Craftiness, Prudence, Wise Strategy

- **Bible Reference:** Proverbs 8:12 – *"I, wisdom, dwell together with prudence (ormah); I possess knowledge and discretion."*

Message: Ormah refers to strategic wisdom—the ability to think ahead and make wise choices. In Proverbs, **ormah** is praised when used righteously but condemned when used deceitfully. Jesus instructed His disciples to be "wise as serpents and innocent as doves," showing that wisdom and integrity go hand in hand. The enemy uses deception, but God gives His people **ormah** to counter the enemy's schemes. Planning wisely and making careful choices prevent unnecessary hardships. Many failures in life come from acting impulsively rather than seeking godly **ormah**. Are you practicing **ormah**, making decisions with wisdom and foresight?

Reflection Questions for the Day:

1. How can strategic wisdom help you avoid pitfalls?

2. Are you planning your steps with godly **ormah**, or are you being reckless?

3. How can you develop discernment to distinguish between wise and deceptive strategies?

Day 274: Tushiyyah (תּוּשִׁיָּה)

- **Meaning:** Sound Wisdom, Practical Counsel, Success Through Wisdom

- **Bible Reference:** Job 12:13 – *"To God belong wisdom (tushiyyah) and power; counsel and understanding are His."*

Message: Tushiyyah represents wisdom that leads to success and stability. While some knowledge is theoretical, **tushiyyah** is practical—it is wisdom that produces good results. Throughout Scripture, those who sought God's **tushiyyah** prospered, while those who rejected it faced destruction. Solomon ruled with **tushiyyah**, making decisions that brought peace and prosperity to Israel. Jesus demonstrated **tushiyyah** in His teachings, providing life-changing counsel that remains relevant today. Seeking **tushiyyah** means asking for wisdom that not only sounds good but works in real life. Are you pursuing wisdom that leads to real transformation, or are you ignoring godly counsel?

Reflection Questions for the Day:

1. What areas of your life need practical wisdom?

2. Are you applying the wisdom you receive, or just hearing it?

3. How can you seek and act upon God's **tushiyyah** in your decisions?

Day 275: Mezimmah (מְ זִ מָּ ה)

- **Meaning:** Purposeful Planning, Wise Counsel, Thoughtfulness

- **Bible Reference:** Proverbs 5:2 – *"That you may maintain discretion (mezimmah) and your lips may preserve knowledge."*

Message: Mezimmah refers to careful thought and planning, ensuring that actions align with godly wisdom. Scripture warns against wicked **mezimmah**, where people scheme for selfish gain. However, righteous **mezimmah** is highly valued, as it leads to good decisions and blessings. Jesus often withdrew to pray before making important decisions, showing the power of thoughtful planning. Many mistakes come from acting without **mezimmah**, failing to consider long-term consequences. God desires for His people to be wise, making choices that honor Him. Are you practicing godly **mezimmah**, planning with wisdom and purpose?

Reflection Questions for the Day:

1. How can wise planning improve your decision-making?

2. Are you seeking godly counsel before making important choices?

3. What steps can you take to develop better foresight in your life?

Day 276: Sod (סוֹד)

- **Meaning:** Secret, Hidden Wisdom, Counsel of God

- **Bible Reference:** Psalm 25:14 – *"The Lord confides (sod) in those who fear Him; He makes His covenant known to them."*

Message: **Sod** refers to deep, hidden wisdom that God reveals to those who seek Him. The Bible says that God shares His secrets with those who fear Him, giving them insight beyond human understanding. Jesus spoke in parables, revealing **sod** only to those with open hearts. Many people seek worldly wisdom but neglect the **sod** of God, missing the deeper truths He wants to reveal. The Holy Spirit gives believers **sod**, opening their eyes to spiritual realities. Seeking **sod** requires humility, a teachable heart, and a deep relationship with God. Are you pursuing the **sod** of God, seeking deeper wisdom in His presence?

Reflection Questions for the Day:

1. How does God reveal hidden wisdom to His people?

2. Are you seeking deeper understanding through prayer and Scripture?

3. What can you do to grow in spiritual insight?

Week 40 Conclusion

This week's words reveal different aspects of divine wisdom. **Sekhel** and **binah** guide our thinking, while **da'at** and **sod** give deeper knowledge. **Ormah** and **mezimmah** help us make wise decisions, and **tushiyyah** ensures our success through godly counsel. True wisdom comes from God, leading to a life of righteousness, clarity, and purpose. When we seek His wisdom, we walk in His light and avoid unnecessary struggles.

Week 41: The Power of God's Protection and Refuge

Day 277: Machseh (מַ֫חְסֶ֫ה)

- **Meaning:** Refuge, Shelter, Safe Haven

- **Bible Reference:** Psalm 91:2 – *"I will say of the Lord, 'He is my refuge (machseh) and my fortress, my God, in whom I trust.'"*

Message: **Machseh** represents a place of safety, where one can find shelter from danger. The Bible describes God as our **machseh**, protecting His people from harm. Life is full of uncertainties, but those who trust in the Lord find security in His presence. Jesus is our ultimate **machseh**, offering peace in the midst of trials. Just as a fortress shields warriors from attack, God's presence surrounds His children with divine protection. Seeking refuge in Him means placing our fears and burdens in His hands. Are you running to God as your **machseh**, or are you looking for security in worldly things?

Reflection Questions for the Day:

1. How do you seek refuge in God during difficult times?

2. Are there fears you need to surrender to God's protection?

3. What can you do to remind yourself that God is your **machseh**?

Day 278: Tzur (צוּר)

- **Meaning:** Rock, Strength, Stability

- **Bible Reference:** Psalm 18:2 – *"The Lord is my rock (tzur), my fortress and my deliverer; my God is my rock, in whom I take refuge."*

Message: Tzur symbolizes God as an unshakable foundation, providing strength and stability. In a world of shifting circumstances, God remains firm, offering His people security. Throughout the Bible, God is called a **tzur**, showing that He is dependable and faithful. Jesus taught that those who build their lives on His words are like wise builders on a rock. When storms come, those who trust in Him stand firm. Human strength and resources fail, but God's **tzur** never wavers. Are you building your life on the solid **tzur**, or are you trusting in things that can be shaken?

Reflection Questions for the Day:

1. What does it mean for God to be your rock?

2. Are you standing firm in faith, or are you shaken by challenges?

3. How can you strengthen your trust in God as your **tzur**?

Day 279: Magen (מָגֵן)

- **Meaning:** Shield, Defender, Protection

- **Bible Reference:** Psalm 3:3 – *"But You, Lord, are a shield (magen) around me, my glory, the One who lifts my head high."*

Message: Magen describes God as a shield, defending His people against danger. Just as a warrior depends on a shield for survival, we rely on God's **magen** to protect us from spiritual attacks. The Bible speaks of the "shield of faith," which guards us from the enemy's schemes. Jesus is our **magen**, covering us with His righteousness and keeping us from harm. When we trust in God, His protection surrounds us, even when we face trials. Walking in faith means believing that God's **magen** is always present. Are you trusting in God's shield, or are you trying to fight battles on your own?

Reflection Questions for the Day:

1. How have you experienced God's protection in your life?

2. Are you using the shield of faith against spiritual attacks?

3. What steps can you take to rely more on God's **magen**?

Day 280: Kanaf (פ,נ,ף)

- **Meaning:** Wing, Covering, Protection

- **Bible Reference:** Psalm 91:4 – *"He will cover you with His feathers, and under His wings (kanaf) you will find refuge."*

Message: Kanaf represents God's protective covering, like a mother bird shielding her chicks. Jesus used this image when He lamented over Jerusalem, desiring to gather His people under His wings. God's **kanaf** is a place of warmth, love, and security, where His children can rest. His protection is not only physical but also spiritual, guarding our hearts and minds. The closer we remain to Him, the more we experience His **kanaf**. Many people run from God's covering, seeking protection elsewhere, only to find themselves vulnerable. Are you resting under God's **kanaf**, allowing Him to shield you?

Reflection Questions for the Day:

1. What does it mean to take refuge under God's wings?

2. Are there times when you have stepped outside of God's protection?

3. How can you stay close to God's **kanaf** in daily life?

Day 281: Misgav (מִ שְׂ גָּ ב)

- **Meaning:** High Tower, Stronghold, Safe Place

- **Bible Reference:** Psalm 62:6 – *"Truly He is my rock and my salvation; He is my fortress (misgav), I will not be shaken."*

Message: Misgav refers to a high, fortified place of protection. Ancient cities had **misgav** towers, providing safety from enemies. God is described as our **misgav**, lifting us above danger and keeping us secure. Jesus is our spiritual **misgav**, shielding us from the attacks of the enemy. Those who dwell in God's **misgav** remain unshaken, even when the world is in turmoil. Climbing to a **misgav** requires effort— seeking God through prayer, worship, and obedience. Are you abiding in God's **misgav**, or are you staying in places of spiritual vulnerability?

Reflection Questions for the Day:

1. What does it mean to dwell in God's **misgav**?

2. How can you position yourself in a place of spiritual safety?

3. Are you relying on God's fortress or trying to protect yourself?

Day 282: Seter (סֵ תֶ ר)

- **Meaning:** Secret Place, Hidden Shelter

- **Bible Reference:** Psalm 91:1 – *"Whoever dwells in the secret place (seter) of the Most High will rest in the shadow of the Almighty."*

Message: Seter represents the intimate, hidden refuge of God's presence. Those who seek Him find rest and protection in His **seter**. The world offers no true security, but those who dwell with God remain safe. Jesus often withdrew to quiet places, demonstrating the importance of seeking God's **seter**. When we prioritize time with God, we experience His peace and protection. The enemy cannot reach those who remain in God's **seter**, as they are covered by His presence. Are you making time to dwell in the **seter** of the Most High?

Reflection Questions for the Day:

1. What does it mean to dwell in God's secret place?

2. How can you cultivate a deeper relationship with God through prayer?

3. Are you spending enough time in God's **seter**, or is your focus elsewhere?

Day 283: Yeshuah (יְשׁוּעָה)

- **Meaning:** Salvation, Deliverance, Rescue

- **Bible Reference:** Isaiah 12:2 – *"Surely God is my salvation (yeshuah); I will trust and not be afraid."*

Message: Yeshuah means salvation, both physical and spiritual. In times of trouble, God provides **yeshuah**, rescuing His people from harm. Jesus is our ultimate **yeshuah**, delivering us from sin and granting us eternal life. Salvation is not just about the afterlife; it is about experiencing God's protection and peace now. When we trust in God's **yeshuah**, we walk in confidence, knowing He is our deliverer. No enemy, fear, or trial can separate us from His saving power. Are you living in the fullness of God's **yeshuah**, trusting Him as your ultimate protector?

Reflection Questions for the Day:

1. How does salvation bring both eternal and present security?

2. Are you fully trusting in God's **yeshuah** in every area of your life?

3. How can you share the message of **yeshuah** with others?

Week 41 Conclusion

This week's words remind us that God is our ultimate place of safety. **Machseh** and **misgav** show that He is our refuge and fortress, while **tzur** and **magen** highlight His strength and defense. **Kanaf** and **seter** emphasize the intimate covering of His presence, and **yeshuah** assures us of His ultimate salvation. True security is found in God alone, not in worldly solutions. When we trust in His protection, we walk in peace and confidence, knowing we are covered by His grace.

Week 42: The Power of God's Presence and Glory

Day 284: Kavod (כָּבוֹד)

- **Meaning:** Glory, Honor, Weightiness of God's Presence

- **Bible Reference:** Psalm 24:8 – *"Who is this King of glory (kavod)? The Lord strong and mighty, the Lord mighty in battle."*

Message: Kavod describes the overwhelming weight and majesty of God's presence. When God's **kavod** filled the temple, the priests could not stand because of its intensity. His glory is not just a bright light or a feeling—it is the manifestation of His power, holiness, and authority. Jesus revealed God's **kavod** on earth, showing His divine nature through miracles, love, and ultimate sacrifice. As believers, we are called to reflect His **kavod**, bringing His presence into the world. Worship, obedience, and humility invite more of God's **kavod** into our lives. Are you seeking to live in God's **kavod**, experiencing His glory daily?

Reflection Questions for the Day:

1. How do you experience God's **kavod** in your life?

2. Are you living in a way that reflects His glory to others?

3. How can you seek more of God's presence in worship?

Day 285: Shekinah (שְׁכִינָה)

- **Meaning:** Dwelling, Manifest Presence of God

- **Bible Reference:** Exodus 40:34 – *"Then the cloud covered the tent of meeting, and the glory of the Lord (Shekinah) filled the tabernacle."*

Message: Shekinah refers to God's indwelling presence among His people. Unlike **kavod**, which emphasizes God's majesty, **Shekinah** speaks of His closeness. In the Old Testament, God's **Shekinah** appeared as a cloud or fire, leading Israel through the wilderness. Jesus was the ultimate revelation of God's **Shekinah**, dwelling among humanity as Emmanuel—"God with us." Today, the Holy Spirit brings the **Shekinah** of God into our hearts, guiding, comforting, and empowering us. When we invite His presence, we become living temples filled with His glory. Are you aware of the **Shekinah** in your life, welcoming God's nearness?

Reflection Questions for the Day:

1. How does knowing God's presence dwells within you change your perspective?

2. Are you making space in your heart for God's **Shekinah**?

3. How can you cultivate a deeper awareness of His presence?

Day 286: Ruach Elohim (רוּחַ אֱלֹהִים)

- **Meaning:** Spirit of God, Divine Breath, Wind

- **Bible Reference:** Genesis 1:2 – *"Now the earth was formless and empty, darkness was over the surface of the deep, and the Spirit of God (Ruach Elohim) was hovering over the waters."*

Message: Ruach Elohim refers to the Spirit of God, His breath that brings life, order, and power. In creation, the **Ruach Elohim** moved over the waters, bringing light and purpose to chaos. The prophets were empowered by the **Ruach Elohim** to proclaim God's truth, and Jesus was anointed by the Spirit for His mission. At Pentecost, the Holy Spirit filled the disciples, marking the beginning of the Church's mission. The same **Ruach Elohim** lives in believers today, empowering them to walk in truth and victory. Are you relying on the power of the **Ruach Elohim**, allowing Him to lead you?

Reflection Questions for the Day:

1. How does the Holy Spirit empower you in your faith?

2. Are you actively seeking the guidance of the **Ruach Elohim** in your daily life?

3. What steps can you take to be more sensitive to the Holy Spirit's leading?

Day 287: Panim (פָּנִים)

- **Meaning:** Face, Presence, Intimacy with God

- **Bible Reference:** Exodus 33:14 – *"The Lord replied, 'My Presence (Panim) will go with you, and I will give you rest.'"*

Message: Panim signifies the presence of God, often translated as "face." To seek God's **Panim** means to desire His nearness, just as Moses longed to see His glory. Sin causes separation from His **Panim**, but through Jesus, we are restored to a face-to-face relationship with Him. The Bible promises that one day, we will see God's **Panim** fully, dwelling with Him in eternity. In prayer and worship, we can already experience His presence, drawing near to Him in spirit. Seeking His **Panim** means prioritizing time with Him and walking in His ways. Are you longing for a deeper experience of God's **Panim** in your life?

Reflection Questions for the Day:

1. How can you seek God's **Panim** more intentionally?

2. Are you making space in your daily life to experience His presence?

3. What habits can you develop to maintain closeness with God?

Day 288: Or (אוֹר)

- **Meaning:** Light, Illumination, Revelation

- **Bible Reference:** Psalm 27:1 – *"The Lord is my light (Or) and my salvation—whom shall I fear?"*

Message: Or represents God's light, which brings clarity, truth, and revelation. Jesus declared, *"I am the Light (Or) of the world,"* showing that He came to dispel darkness and lead people into truth. God's **Or** exposes sin but also reveals His grace, guiding us into righteousness. The world is full of deception, but those who walk in God's **Or** will not stumble. Believers are called to reflect His **Or**, shining His truth in a dark world. The more we abide in His Word, the more His **Or** fills our hearts. Are you walking in the **Or** of God, allowing Him to illuminate your path?

Reflection Questions for the Day:

1. How does God's light guide you in difficult situations?

2. Are you reflecting His **Or** to those around you?

3. How can you spend more time in God's Word to receive His illumination?

Day 289: Shakan (שָׁכַן)

- **Meaning:** To Dwell, To Settle, To Abide

- **Bible Reference:** Psalm 37:3 – *"Trust in the Lord and do good; dwell (Shakan) in the land and enjoy safe pasture."*

Message: Shakan means to dwell or abide, reflecting God's desire to be close to His people. The tabernacle (Mishkan) was the place where God's presence **Shakan** among Israel. Jesus came to "dwell among us," showing God's longing for intimacy with humanity. Through the Holy Spirit, God now **Shakan** within every believer, making our hearts His home. True peace and security come when we choose to **Shakan** in His presence, not just visit Him occasionally. Abiding in Him means seeking Him daily, not just in emergencies. Are you allowing God to **Shakan** in your life, or are you keeping Him at a distance?

Reflection Questions for the Day:

1. What does it mean to dwell in God's presence?

2. Are you actively abiding in Christ, or just visiting Him occasionally?

3. How can you develop a deeper relationship where God's presence **Shakan** in your life?

Week 42 Conclusion

This week's words highlight different aspects of God's presence. **Kavod** and **Shekinah** reveal His glory, while **Ruach Elohim** brings life and power. **Panim** speaks of intimacy, and **Or** illuminates our paths. **Shakan** reminds us that God desires to dwell with us continually. Walking in His presence transforms our lives, bringing peace, wisdom, and strength. May we seek Him daily, longing for His **Panim**, filled with His **Or**, and abiding in His **Shakan** forever.

Week 43: The Power of God's Grace and Mercy

Day 290: Chen (חֵן)

- **Meaning:** Grace, Favor, Kindness

- **Bible Reference:** Proverbs 3:34 – *"He mocks proud mockers but shows favor (chen) to the humble and oppressed."*

Message: Chen refers to the unmerited favor and grace of God, given freely to those who seek Him. Grace is not something we can earn—it is a gift from God's love and kindness. Throughout the Bible, people like Noah, Joseph, and Esther found **chen** in the sight of God and others, leading to their blessings and protection. Jesus is the ultimate expression of God's **chen**, offering salvation through His sacrifice. His grace enables us to walk in righteousness, not by our own strength but through His Spirit. When we humble ourselves, we position ourselves to receive His **chen**. Are you living in God's grace, or are you trying to earn His favor through your own efforts?

Reflection Questions for the Day:

1. How have you experienced God's grace in your life?

2. Are you fully accepting His **chen**, or are you relying on your own works?

3. How can you extend grace to others as God has shown it to you?

Day 291: Rachamim (רַחֲמִים)

- **Meaning:** Compassion, Tender Mercy, Deep Affection

- **Bible Reference:** Lamentations 3:22 – *"Because of the Lord's great love (rachamim) we are not consumed, for His compassions never fail."*

Message: **Rachamim** comes from the root *rechem*, meaning "womb," symbolizing the deep, nurturing love God has for His children. God's **rachamim** is seen throughout Scripture as He repeatedly forgives and restores His people. Jesus embodied **rachamim**, healing the sick, welcoming sinners, and showing mercy to those who least deserved it. His compassion led Him to the cross, where He made the ultimate sacrifice for our sins. We are called to show **rachamim** to others, reflecting God's mercy in our relationships. When we receive His mercy, we are transformed to be merciful ourselves. Are you extending God's **rachamim** to others, or are you quick to judge?

Reflection Questions for the Day:

1. How have you experienced God's mercy in your life?

2. Are you willing to show **rachamim** to those who have wronged you?

3. How can you cultivate a heart that reflects God's compassion?

Day 292: Selichah (ס. ל. יח. ה)

- **Meaning:** Forgiveness, Pardon, Release from Guilt

- **Bible Reference:** Psalm 130:4 – *"But with You there is forgiveness (selichah), so that we can, with reverence, serve You."*

Message: **Selichah** is God's gift of forgiveness, releasing us from sin and restoring us to fellowship with Him. True

selichah is not just about excusing wrongs but about restoring relationships. The Bible teaches that God is abundant in **selichah**, always willing to forgive those who repent. Jesus emphasized **selichah** when He taught His followers to forgive others as God has forgiven them. Holding onto unforgiveness hinders our spiritual growth, while extending **selichah** brings freedom and healing. Accepting God's **selichah** means also offering it to others, reflecting His love and grace. Are you holding onto past hurts, or are you embracing God's call to forgive?

Reflection Questions for the Day:

1. Have you fully received God's forgiveness in your life?

2. Are you willing to forgive others as God has forgiven you?

3. How can you practice **selichah** daily in your relationships?

Day 293: Kapparah (כַּ_פָּ_רָ_ה)

- **Meaning:** Atonement, Covering, Reconciliation

- **Bible Reference:** Leviticus 17:11 – *"For the life of a creature is in the blood, and I have given it to you to make atonement (kapparah) for yourselves on the altar."*

Message: Kapparah refers to the act of atonement, covering sin and restoring broken relationships with God. In the Old Testament, sacrifices were made as **kapparah**, symbolizing the need for purification. Jesus became our ultimate **kapparah**, shedding His blood once and for all to cleanse us from sin. His atonement is not temporary but eternal, granting us access to the Father. Because of His **kapparah**, we no longer need to live in guilt or separation. Accepting His atonement means walking in freedom, knowing we are fully reconciled with God. Are you living in the fullness of Christ's **kapparah**, or are you still carrying the weight of sin?

Reflection Questions for the Day:

1. What does Jesus' atonement mean for your relationship with God?

2. Are you fully embracing the freedom that comes with His **kapparah**?

3. How can you help others understand the power of Jesus' sacrifice?

Day 294: Nacham (נ‎,ח‎,ם)

- **Meaning:** To Comfort, To Relent, To Show Compassion

- **Bible Reference:** Isaiah 49:13 – *"The Lord comforts (nacham) His people and will have compassion on His afflicted ones."*

Message: Nacham describes God's deep desire to comfort His people in times of sorrow and distress. Throughout Scripture, we see God bringing **nacham** to those who are brokenhearted. Jesus declared that those who mourn would be comforted, emphasizing God's tender care for His children. The Holy Spirit is called the Comforter, continuing God's work of **nacham** in our lives. When we seek Him, He replaces sorrow with joy and despair with hope. Just as we receive **nacham**, we are called to be a source of comfort to others. Are you allowing God's **nacham** to heal your heart, and are you sharing that comfort with others?

Reflection Questions for the Day:

1. How has God comforted you in difficult times?

2. Are you making space for the Holy Spirit to bring **nacham** into your life?

3. How can you be a source of comfort to those around you?

Day 295: Chanan (חָנַן)

- **Meaning:** To Be Gracious, Show Favor, Bestow Mercy

- **Bible Reference:** Numbers 6:25 – *"The Lord make His face shine on you and be gracious (chanan) to you."*

Message: Chanan describes God's graciousness, His willingness to bless us beyond what we deserve. Grace is more than just mercy—it is unearned kindness poured out on us. The Bible is filled with examples of God's **chanan**, from His provision for Israel to the ultimate gift of salvation through Jesus. Jesus embodied **chanan**, extending grace to sinners, healing the broken, and welcoming the outcast. As recipients of God's **chanan**, we are called to reflect His grace in how we treat others. Grace should define our actions, speech, and relationships. Are you extending **chanan** to others as freely as God has given it to you?

Reflection Questions for the Day:

1. What does it mean for God to be gracious to you?

2. Are you extending grace to others in your daily life?

3. How can you grow in being a more gracious person?

Week 43 Conclusion

This week's words remind us of the deep, unshakable grace and mercy of God. **Chen** reveals His unmerited favor, while **rachamim** and **selichah** highlight His compassion and forgiveness. **Kapparah** shows the atonement through Christ, and **nacham** assures us of His comfort. **Chanan** calls us to reflect God's grace in our own lives. Living in God's mercy means walking in freedom, extending His love to others, and trusting in His unfailing goodness. May we never take His grace for granted but instead share it abundantly.

Week 44: The Power of God's Holiness and Purity

Day 296: Qadosh (קָדוֹשׁ)

- **Meaning:** Holy, Set Apart, Sacred

- **Bible Reference:** Isaiah 6:3 – *"Holy (qadosh), holy, holy is the Lord Almighty; the whole earth is full of His glory."*

Message: Qadosh means "holy" and emphasizes God's absolute purity and separateness from sin. In Isaiah's vision, the seraphim declared God's **qadosh** three times, showing the perfection of His holiness. God calls His people to be **qadosh**, to be set apart for His purposes. Holiness is not just about following rules but about aligning our hearts with God's will. Jesus, the Holy One, demonstrated **qadosh** by living a life of complete obedience to the Father. Walking in holiness requires daily surrender, choosing righteousness over sin. Are you pursuing holiness in your thoughts, words, and actions?

Reflection Questions for the Day:

1. What does it mean to be holy as God is holy?

2. Are there areas in your life that need to be surrendered to God's holiness?

3. How can you reflect God's holiness in your daily walk?

Day 297: Tahor (טָהוֹר)

- **Meaning:** Pure, Clean, Uncontaminated

- **Bible Reference:** Psalm 51:10 – *"Create in me a pure (tahor) heart, O God, and renew a steadfast spirit within me."*

Message: Tahor represents purity, both physical and spiritual. In the Old Testament, rituals were established to maintain ceremonial **tahor**, but Jesus emphasized the need for inner purity. A **tahor** heart is not just free from outward sin but is aligned with God's desires. True **tahor** comes from seeking God, confessing sins, and living in His truth. The world promotes impurity, but God calls His people to be spiritually clean. Jesus' sacrifice made it possible for us to be **tahor**, washing away our sins completely. Are you allowing God to purify your heart and mind?

Reflection Questions for the Day:

1. What areas of your life need spiritual cleansing?

2. Are you guarding your heart against impurity?

3. How can you cultivate a **tahor** heart before God?

Day 298: Tamim (תָּמִים)

- **Meaning:** Blameless, Whole, Complete, Without Defect

- **Bible Reference:** Deuteronomy 18:13 – *"You must be blameless (tamim) before the Lord your God."*

Message: Tamim means being whole and complete, without moral or spiritual corruption. God desires His people to walk in **tamim**, living with integrity and uprightness. Noah was described as **tamim**, a man who walked faithfully with God in a corrupt generation. Jesus, the perfect Lamb, was **tamim**, without sin or blemish, making Him the ultimate sacrifice. Living **tamim** does not mean being perfect but striving for sincerity and truth in our relationship with God. God sees the heart and calls us to live blamelessly before Him. Are you walking in **tamim**, living with integrity and wholehearted devotion to God?

Reflection Questions for the Day:

1. What does it mean to live blamelessly before God?

2. Are there areas of compromise in your life that need to be addressed?

3. How can you grow in spiritual integrity and wholeness?

Day 299: Nazir (נָזִיר)

- **Meaning:** Consecrated, Dedicated, Set Apart for God

- **Bible Reference:** Numbers 6:2 – *"If a man or woman wants to make a special vow, a vow of dedication (nazir) to the Lord as a Nazirite..."*

Message: Nazir refers to someone consecrated or set apart for God's purposes. Nazirites like Samson and Samuel took vows to live differently, showing complete devotion to the Lord. While not everyone is called to take a Nazirite vow, all believers are called to live consecrated lives. Being **nazir** means separating from sin and dedicating yourself to holiness. Jesus lived as the ultimate example of consecration, fully dedicated to the Father's will. Modern believers are called to live as **nazir**, prioritizing God's kingdom over worldly distractions. Are you living a life that is truly set apart for God?

Reflection Questions for the Day:

1. What does it mean to be set apart for God?

2. Are there distractions pulling you away from full devotion to Him?

3. How can you live in greater consecration to God's purposes?

Day 300: Mikveh (מ. ק. ו. ה)

- **Meaning:** Gathering of Waters, Ritual Cleansing, Hope

- **Bible Reference:** Jeremiah 17:13 – *"Lord, You are the hope (mikveh) of Israel; all who forsake You will be put to shame."*

Message: Mikveh originally referred to a collection of water used for ritual purification, symbolizing cleansing and renewal. Over time, it also became a symbol of hope—just as water restores physically, God restores spiritually. Baptism in the New Testament reflects the concept of **mikveh**, representing rebirth and purification through Christ. Just as the waters of the **mikveh** washed away impurity, Jesus' blood cleanses us from sin. True hope (**mikveh**) is found in God alone, not in human efforts or temporary solutions. Coming to God for spiritual cleansing restores joy and peace. Are you seeking God's **mikveh**, allowing Him to cleanse and renew you?

Reflection Questions for the Day:

1. What areas of your life need spiritual renewal?

2. Are you placing your hope (**mikveh**) in God or in temporary things?

3. How can you daily walk in the cleansing power of Christ?

316

Day 301: Yare (יָ ר אַ)

- **Meaning:** Reverence, Fear of the Lord, Awe

- **Bible Reference:** Proverbs 9:10 – *"The fear (yare) of the Lord is the beginning of wisdom, and knowledge of the Holy One is understanding."*

Message: Yare means having deep reverence and awe for God, recognizing His holiness and power. The Bible teaches that **yare** is the foundation of wisdom, leading to obedience and righteousness. Many misunderstand the fear of the Lord, but it is not about terror—it is about honoring Him above all else. Jesus lived with perfect **yare**, always submitting to the Father's will. When we have a proper **yare** of God, we avoid sin and draw closer to Him in worship. A heart that truly fears God walks in wisdom, peace, and joy. Are you cultivating a deeper **yare**, honoring God in all you do?

Reflection Questions for the Day:

1. How do you view the fear of the Lord?

2. Are you living in reverence, honoring God in all areas of your life?

3. How can a deeper **yare** lead to wisdom and obedience?

Day 302: Kedushah (קְ דוּשׁ הָ)

- **Meaning:** Holiness, Sanctification, Sacredness

- **Bible Reference:** Leviticus 20:7 – *"Consecrate yourselves and be holy (kedushah), because I am the Lord your God."*

Message: Kedushah signifies holiness, the process of being sanctified and set apart for God. While **qadosh** describes God's holiness, **kedushah** refers to the holiness we are called to pursue. God desires His people to live in **kedushah**, being transformed daily into His image. Sanctification is a lifelong journey, requiring surrender, obedience, and intimacy with God. Jesus prayed for His followers to be sanctified in truth, set apart for the Father's glory. Walking in **kedushah** brings joy, purpose, and deeper fellowship with God. Are you actively seeking to grow in **kedushah**, becoming more like Christ?

Reflection Questions for the Day:

1. What areas of your life need greater holiness?

2. Are you allowing God to sanctify you through His Word?

3. How can you walk in **kedushah**, set apart for God's purposes?

Week 44 Conclusion

This week's words reveal God's call to holiness. **Qadosh** and **kedushah** remind us of His purity, while **tahor** and **tamim** call us to live blamelessly. **Nazir** challenges us to consecrate our lives, and **mikveh** invites us into renewal and hope. **Yare** reminds us that true wisdom begins with reverence for God. Living in holiness leads to a deeper relationship with Him, transforming us to reflect His character. May we pursue purity, surrendering our hearts fully to the Lord.

Week 45: The Power of God's Restoration and Renewal

Day 303: Shuv (שׁוּב)

- **Meaning:** To Return, To Repent, To Restore

- **Bible Reference:** Joel 2:13 – *"Return (shuv) to the Lord your God, for He is gracious and compassionate, slow to anger and abounding in love."*

Message: Shuv means to turn back, often referring to repentance and returning to God. Throughout the Bible, God calls His people to **shuv**, urging them to leave their sinful ways and come back to Him. The story of the prodigal son illustrates **shuv**, as the son realized his mistake and returned to his father's loving embrace. True repentance is more than just saying sorry—it is a transformation of the heart. God promises restoration to those who **shuv**, offering mercy and renewal. Jesus came to call sinners to **shuv**, providing the way for reconciliation with the Father. Are you living a life of **shuv**, constantly returning to God's presence?

Reflection Questions for the Day:

1. What does it mean to truly repent and turn back to God?

2. Are there areas in your life where you need to **shuv**?

3. How does God's mercy encourage you to return to Him daily?

Day 304: Chadesh (חָ דָ שׁ)

- **Meaning:** To Renew, To Restore, To Make New

- **Bible Reference:** Psalm 51:10 – *"Create in me a pure heart, O God, and renew (chadesh) a steadfast spirit within me."*

Message: Chadesh represents God's power to bring renewal and restoration. When David sinned, he cried out for God to **chadesh** his heart, seeking a fresh start. God specializes in renewal, taking what is broken and making it whole again. Jesus offers new life to all who come to Him, bringing spiritual rebirth. The Bible promises that God's mercies are **chadesh** every morning, meaning His grace is always available. We are not bound by our past—through Christ, we can be made new. Are you allowing God to **chadesh** your heart and spirit daily?

Reflection Questions for the Day:

1. What areas of your life need renewal?

2. Are you holding onto the past instead of embracing God's **chadesh**?

3. How can you live in the daily renewal of God's grace?

Day 305: Rapha (רָפָא)

- **Meaning:** To Heal, To Restore, To Make Whole

- **Bible Reference:** Exodus 15:26 – *"I am the Lord who heals (rapha) you."*

Message: Rapha refers to God's power to heal physically, emotionally, and spiritually. Throughout Scripture, God reveals Himself as Jehovah-Rapha, the Lord who heals. Jesus' ministry was filled with acts of **rapha**, restoring the sick, the broken, and the outcasts. God's healing is not just about the body—it is about restoring hearts, relationships, and faith. When we bring our wounds to God, He is faithful to bring **rapha**, renewing us from the inside out. Healing sometimes requires patience, but God's promises remain true. Are you trusting God for His **rapha**, allowing Him to restore you completely?

Reflection Questions for the Day:

1. What areas of your life need God's healing touch?

2. Are you willing to trust God's timing in your healing process?

3. How can you help others experience God's **rapha**?

Day 306: Komeimiyut (קוֹמְ.מִ.יוּת)

- **Meaning:** Restoration, Uplifting, Standing Tall Again

- **Bible Reference:** Leviticus 26:13 – *"I broke the bars of your yoke and enabled you to walk upright (komeimiyut)."*

Message: Komeimiyut describes the act of rising again, standing tall after being broken or oppressed. God desires to lift up His people, restoring their dignity and strength. When Israel was in captivity, He promised to bring **komeimiyut**, freeing them to stand in His righteousness. Jesus restored those who had been cast down, giving them new purpose and hope. God does not leave us in our brokenness—He lifts us up and restores our identity in Him. Walking in **komeimiyut** means embracing God's restoration and standing firm in His promises. Are you allowing God to lift you up, or are you holding onto past burdens?

Reflection Questions for the Day:

1. What does it mean to walk in God's restoration?

2. Are you embracing the freedom God has given you, or still living in past struggles?

322

3. How can you help others find **komeimiyut** in Christ?

Day 307: Shalom (שָׁ,לוֹם)

- **Meaning:** Peace, Wholeness, Harmony, Complete Restoration

- **Bible Reference:** Isaiah 26:3 – *"You will keep in perfect peace (shalom) those whose minds are steadfast, because they trust in You."*

Message: Shalom is more than just the absence of conflict—it means complete well-being, restoration, and peace with God. When Jesus said, *"My peace (shalom) I give to you,"* He was offering total restoration for our souls. True **shalom** is found in trusting God, knowing He is in control. The world offers temporary peace, but God's **shalom** is lasting, bringing deep joy and security. Resting in **shalom** means surrendering worries, trusting His plans, and walking in His presence. Jesus is the Prince of **Shalom**, bringing healing and completeness to all who follow Him. Are you living in the fullness of God's **shalom**, or are you consumed by stress and fear?

Reflection Questions for the Day:

1. How do you seek God's **shalom** in your daily life?

2. Are you allowing anxiety to steal your peace?

3. How can you help bring God's **shalom** into the lives of others?

Day 308: Tikvah (תָּ,קָ,וָ,ה)

- **Meaning:** Hope, Expectation, Trust in God's Future

- **Bible Reference:** Jeremiah 29:11 – *"For I know the plans I have for you, declares the Lord, plans to prosper you and not to harm you, plans to give you hope (tikvah) and a future."*

Message: Tikvah represents hope that is anchored in God's faithfulness. Biblical hope is not just wishful thinking—it is a confident expectation that God will fulfill His promises. The Israelites held onto **tikvah** during exile, knowing God would restore them. Jesus is our greatest **tikvah**, offering eternal life and victory over sin. When we place our **tikvah** in Him, we are never disappointed. Even in difficult seasons, hope in God brings strength and endurance. Are you holding onto **tikvah**, trusting in God's future for you?

Reflection Questions for the Day:

1. What are you hoping for in God's promises?

2. Are you placing your **tikvah** in circumstances, or in God's faithfulness?

3. How can you encourage others to have hope in Christ?

Week 45 Conclusion

This week's words remind us of God's ability to restore and renew all things. **Shuv** calls us to repentance, while **chadesh** brings renewal. **Rapha** speaks of healing, and **komeimiyut** assures us of restoration. **Shalom** offers complete wholeness, and **tikvah** gives us confident hope for the future. God is a God of new beginnings, bringing life and renewal to all who seek Him. No matter what we have lost, God's restoring power is greater. May we walk in His renewal, trusting in His perfect plan.

Week 46: The Power of God's Faithfulness and Promises

Day 309: Emun (אֱמוּן)

- **Meaning:** Faithfulness, Stability, Firmness

- **Bible Reference:** Deuteronomy 32:4 – *"He is the Rock, His works are perfect, and all His ways are just. A faithful (emun) God who does no wrong, upright and just is He."*

Message: Emun describes God's unwavering faithfulness and reliability. Unlike people who can change or fail, God remains constant in His promises. Throughout Scripture, He has shown His **emun**, from delivering Israel to fulfilling His covenant through Jesus. Faithfulness is one of God's defining characteristics, assuring us that He will never abandon us. Because God is faithful, we can trust His Word and His plans for our lives. His faithfulness calls us to respond in trust and obedience. Are you relying on God's **emun**, standing firm in His promises even when circumstances seem uncertain?

Reflection Questions for the Day:

1. How have you seen God's faithfulness in your life?

2. Are you trusting in God's **emun**, even in difficult times?

3. How can you grow in faithfulness to God and others?

Day 310: Dabar (דָּבָר)

- **Meaning:** Word, Promise, Decree

- **Bible Reference:** Isaiah 55:11 – *"So is My word (dabar) that goes out from My mouth: It will not return to Me empty, but will accomplish what I desire and achieve the purpose for which I sent it."*

Message: Dabar represents the spoken word of God, which carries power and authority. When God speaks, His **dabar** is not just information—it is an active force that brings change. His promises are sure, and His words never fail. Jesus, as the living **Dabar** (Word), fulfilled the Scriptures and demonstrated God's truth in action. Many people doubt God's promises, but His **dabar** never returns void. When we stand on God's Word, we build our lives on a firm foundation. Are you holding onto God's **dabar**, trusting that His promises will be fulfilled?

Reflection Questions for the Day:

1. What promises of God are you standing on today?

2. How can you apply God's **dabar** in your daily life?

3. Are you speaking God's Word in faith over your circumstances?

Day 311: Zecher (זֵ כֶ ר)

- **Meaning:** Remembrance, Memorial, Legacy

- **Bible Reference:** Psalm 77:11 – *"I will remember (zecher) the deeds of the Lord; yes, I will remember Your miracles of long ago."*

Message: Zecher refers to remembering God's past faithfulness as a foundation for trusting Him in the present. Throughout the Bible, God commands His people to set up memorials as reminders of His works. Forgetting leads to fear and doubt, but remembering builds faith and gratitude. Jesus established the Lord's Supper as a **zecher**, calling us to remember His sacrifice. When we reflect on God's past deeds, we gain confidence in His future promises. Writing down testimonies and sharing them with others strengthens our faith. Are you keeping a **zecher** of God's faithfulness, reminding yourself of His goodness?

Reflection Questions for the Day:

1. What past victories can you remember that show God's faithfulness?

2. How can you develop a habit of remembering God's goodness?

3. Are you sharing your testimonies with others to strengthen their faith?

Day 312: Oath (שְׁ בוּעָ ה)

- **Meaning:** Oath, Vow, Binding Promise

- **Bible Reference:** Hebrews 6:17 – *"Because God wanted to make the unchanging nature of His purpose very clear to the heirs of what was promised, He confirmed it with an oath (oath)."*

Message: Oath refers to a solemn vow or binding promise, something that God takes seriously. In the Bible, God made oaths to His people, swearing by His own name because there is no one greater. His oath to Abraham was fulfilled through Jesus, demonstrating His faithfulness to keep His word. Unlike human promises that can be broken, God's **oath** is unchangeable and eternal. This gives us confidence in His salvation and His commitment to us. As believers, we are also called to be people of integrity, keeping our words and commitments. Are you trusting in God's unbreakable **oath**, and are you honoring your own commitments?

Reflection Questions for the Day:

1. How does knowing God keeps His promises strengthen your faith?

2. Are you honoring your own commitments with integrity?

3. What oaths or vows have you made before God that you need to fulfill?

Day 313: Ahuzzah (אֲחֻזָּה)

- **Meaning:** Possession, Inheritance, Land of Promise

- **Bible Reference:** Genesis 17:8 – *"The whole land of Canaan, where you now reside as a foreigner, I will give as an everlasting possession (ahuzzah) to you and your descendants after you."*

Message: Ahuzzah represents the inheritance that God promises to His people. In the Old Testament, He gave Israel the land of Canaan as their **ahuzzah**, fulfilling His covenant with Abraham. In the New Testament, our **ahuzzah** is the kingdom of God and the eternal life given through Christ. Many people focus on temporary possessions, but God's **ahuzzah** is everlasting and far greater than earthly treasures. Jesus told His followers to seek their inheritance in heaven rather than in material wealth. As heirs with Christ, we have a divine **ahuzzah** that cannot be taken away. Are you pursuing God's eternal **ahuzzah**, or are you chasing after temporary rewards?

Reflection Questions for the Day:

1. What does your heavenly inheritance mean to you?

2. Are you prioritizing eternal rewards over temporary possessions?

330

3. How can you live in a way that reflects your **ahuzzah** in Christ?

Day 314: Immanu (עִ מָ נוּ)

- **Meaning:** With Us, Near to Us

- **Bible Reference:** Isaiah 7:14 – *"The virgin will conceive and give birth to a son, and will call Him Immanuel (Immanu-El) – 'God with us.'"*

Message: Immanu signifies God's nearness, a truth that brings comfort and assurance. Throughout the Bible, God reassured His people with His presence, saying, *"I am with you."* Jesus, as Immanuel, fulfilled this promise by coming to dwell among humanity. Even after His ascension, He sent the Holy Spirit to be **Immanu**, with us always. When we feel abandoned or alone, remembering God's **Immanu** gives us strength. His presence is not based on our emotions but on His unchanging promise. Are you living with the awareness that God is **Immanu**, always with you?

Reflection Questions for the Day:

1. How does knowing God is always with you change your perspective?

2. Are you actively seeking His presence in your daily life?

3. How can you remind yourself of God's **Immanu** in difficult times?

Week 46 Conclusion

This week's words highlight the unshakable nature of God's faithfulness. **Emun** assures us that He never fails, while **dabar** confirms that His Word always accomplishes His purposes. **Zecher** calls us to remember His past works, and **oath** reminds us that His promises are unbreakable. **Ahuzzah** points to our eternal inheritance, and **Immanu** assures us that He is always with us. Trusting in God's faithfulness leads to a life of peace, security, and confidence in His plans. May we stand firm on His promises and live in the certainty of His presence.

Week 47: The Power of God's Leadership and Guidance

Day 315: Derekh (דֶּרֶךְ)

- **Meaning:** Way, Path, Journey

- **Bible Reference:** Proverbs 3:6 – *"In all your ways (derekh) submit to Him, and He will make your paths straight."*

Message: Derekh refers to the path one walks, symbolizing life's journey and the direction we choose. The Bible often speaks of following God's **derekh**, which leads to life, while straying from it leads to destruction. Jesus declared, *"I am the way (derekh), the truth, and the life,"* revealing that He is the only path to the Father. Walking in God's **derekh** requires trust, obedience, and alignment with His Word. Sometimes, His way may not seem clear, but faith calls us to follow even when we cannot see. The world's paths may seem attractive, but they lead to emptiness—only God's **derekh** brings true purpose. Are you walking in God's **derekh**, allowing Him to guide your steps?

Reflection Questions for the Day:

1. Are you following God's path or your own?

2. How can you ensure that your daily choices align with God's **derekh**?

3. What distractions may be leading you away from His way?

Day 316: Yashar (יָשָׁר)

- **Meaning:** Straight, Upright, Righteous Path

- **Bible Reference:** Psalm 25:8 – *"Good and upright (yashar) is the Lord; therefore He instructs sinners in His ways."*

Message: Yashar refers to the straight and upright way, symbolizing a life of righteousness and moral integrity. The Lord is **yashar**, and He calls His people to walk in integrity and truth. In a world full of deception and compromise, staying on the **yashar** path requires commitment to God's commands. The righteous do not seek shortcuts or crooked ways but trust that God's **yashar** path leads to true success. Jesus walked the **yashar** path perfectly, providing an example for us to follow. Choosing the upright way may not always be easy, but it brings lasting rewards. Are you committed to walking in the **yashar** path of righteousness?

Reflection Questions for the Day:

1. What does it mean to walk uprightly before God?

2. Are there areas in your life where you are tempted to take shortcuts?

3. How can you strengthen your integrity and commitment to the **yashar** path?

Day 317: Hazon (חָזוֹן)

- **Meaning:** Vision, Revelation, Divine Insight

- **Bible Reference:** Proverbs 29:18 – *"Where there is no vision (hazon), the people perish; but blessed is the one who heeds wisdom's instruction."*

Message: Hazon refers to prophetic vision and divine revelation, the ability to see God's purposes clearly. Without **hazon**, people lose direction, wandering aimlessly without knowing their purpose. God gives **hazon** to those who seek Him, revealing His plans through Scripture, prayer, and the Holy Spirit. Jesus came to give us **hazon**, opening our eyes to the kingdom of God and His will for our lives. Having **hazon**

means not just seeing, but acting on what God reveals. Without vision, we settle for mediocrity, but with **hazon**, we walk boldly in our calling. Are you seeking God's **hazon**, asking Him to reveal His plans for your life?

Reflection Questions for the Day:

1. Do you have a clear vision of God's purpose for your life?

2. Are you spending time in prayer and Scripture to seek divine insight?

3. How can you align your actions with God's **hazon** for your life?

Day 318: Tov (טוֹב)

- **Meaning:** Good, Pleasant, Beneficial

- **Bible Reference:** Psalm 34:8 – *"Taste and see that the Lord is good (tov); blessed is the one who takes refuge in Him."*

Message: Tov describes the goodness of God and His plans for His people. From creation, everything God made was declared **tov**, reflecting His perfect nature. Jesus, the Good Shepherd, leads His people in **tov** paths, providing and protecting them. Even in trials, God's **tov** is working for our ultimate good, shaping us into His image. Trusting in His goodness means believing that His ways are always better than our own. We are called to reflect His **tov**, bringing His goodness into the world through our words and actions. Are you trusting in God's **tov**, even when life is uncertain?

Reflection Questions for the Day:

1. How have you experienced God's goodness in your life?

2. Are you reflecting His **tov** in your interactions with others?

3. How can you trust in God's goodness, even in difficult situations?

Day 319: Yad (ד,י)

- **Meaning:** Hand, Power, Strength

- **Bible Reference:** Isaiah 41:10 – *"I will strengthen you and help you; I will uphold you with My righteous right hand (yad)."*

Message: Yad represents God's hand, symbolizing His power, guidance, and provision. Throughout Scripture, God's **yad** led His people, performing mighty miracles and delivering them from trouble. The Bible speaks of God's righteous **yad**, upholding and protecting those who trust in Him. Jesus demonstrated the **yad** of God, healing the sick and lifting the broken. God's hand is always at work, even when we do not see it. Trusting in His **yad** means surrendering control, believing that He holds our future. Are you placing your life in God's **yad**, allowing Him to lead and strengthen you?

Reflection Questions for the Day:

1. How have you seen God's **yad** guiding your life?

2. Are you fully surrendering to God's power and direction?

3. How can you trust in God's **yad** more deeply in your daily walk?

Day 320: Pequddah (פְּ.קֻ.דָּ.ה)

- **Meaning:** Visitation, Divine Oversight, God's Appointed Time

- **Bible Reference:** Luke 19:44 – *"They will not leave one stone on another, because you did not recognize the time of God's visitation (pequddah)."*

Message: Pequddah speaks of God's divine appointment and oversight, a specific time when He acts in history and in our lives. Throughout Scripture, God visited His people at crucial moments, bringing judgment, blessing, or deliverance. Jesus lamented over Jerusalem because they failed to recognize their **pequddah,** the time of their divine visitation. Today, God continues to move in appointed seasons, guiding His people in His perfect timing. Recognizing His **pequddah** requires spiritual awareness, prayer, and readiness to act. We must not miss God's appointed moments due to distraction or unbelief. Are you prepared for God's **pequddah,** recognizing when He is calling you to act?

Reflection Questions for the Day:

1. Are you spiritually aware of God's appointed moments in your life?

2. How can you prepare yourself to recognize and respond to God's **pequddah**?

3. Are there past moments where you felt God visited your life in a powerful way?

Week 47 Conclusion

This week's words remind us of God's guidance and leadership in our lives. **Derekh** shows that God directs our paths, while **yashar** calls us to walk uprightly. **Hazon** gives us vision and direction, and **tov** assures us of His goodness. **Yad** represents His hand of power, while **pequddah** reveals His divine timing. Trusting in God's leadership means surrendering to His plans, seeking His vision, and walking in His ways. When we follow His direction, we live with confidence, knowing we are on the path He has designed for us. May we always be aware of His presence, responding to His guidance with faith and obedience.

Week 48: The Power of God's Strength and Victory

Day 321: Gibbor (גִּבּוֹר)

- **Meaning:** Mighty, Warrior, Champion

- **Bible Reference:** Isaiah 9:6 – *"For to us a child is born, to us a son is given... and He will be called Mighty God (El Gibbor), Everlasting Father, Prince of Peace."*

Message: Gibbor describes someone who is strong, courageous, and victorious. God is often referred to as **El Gibbor**, the Mighty God, who fights for His people and wins their battles. In the Old Testament, many leaders, like David, were called **gibbor** because of their bravery in battle, but ultimate victory comes from God alone. Jesus, as **El Gibbor**, conquered sin, death, and the enemy, proving that true strength comes from God's power. As believers, we are called to be **gibbor** in our faith, standing firm in trials and fighting the good fight. Spiritual battles are won not by human strength but by relying on God's might. Are you walking in God's strength, trusting Him to be your **gibbor**?

Reflection Questions for the Day:

1. How have you seen God as a mighty warrior in your life?

2. Are you relying on your own strength or on God's power?

3. What battles in your life do you need to surrender to **El Gibbor**?

Day 322: Oz (עֹז)

- **Meaning:** Strength, Power, Might

- **Bible Reference:** Psalm 28:7 – *"The Lord is my strength (oz) and my shield; my heart trusts in Him, and He helps me."*

Message: Oz represents a deep, unshakable strength that comes from God. Many seek strength in wealth, power, or human ability, but true **oz** is found in the Lord. David, a warrior king, understood that victory was not in his military skill but in God's **oz**. Jesus displayed divine **oz**, standing firm in obedience to the Father, even unto death. When we trust in God's strength, we find peace even in trials. The world's definition of strength is self-reliance, but God calls us to depend on Him completely. Are you drawing your **oz** from God, or are you trusting in your own ability?

Reflection Questions for the Day:

1. What does it mean to rely on God's **oz** rather than your own?

2. How can you cultivate spiritual strength through faith?

3. Are you allowing God's **oz** to sustain you in difficult seasons?

Day 323: Teshuah (תְּשׁוּעָה)

- **Meaning:** Deliverance, Salvation, Victory

- **Bible Reference:** 2 Samuel 22:2 – *"The Lord is my rock, my fortress, and my deliverer (teshuah)."*

Message: Teshuah describes the act of being rescued or saved, whether from enemies, sin, or trouble. Throughout the Bible, God brings **teshuah** to His people, delivering them from bondage, battle, and destruction. Jesus brought the ultimate **teshuah** through His death and resurrection, rescuing humanity from sin. Victory is not something we achieve alone—it is given to us by God's power. Even in spiritual battles, we fight from victory, not for victory, because Jesus has already won. Trusting in God's **teshuah** means surrendering control and believing that He is our rescuer. Are you walking in the confidence of God's **teshuah**, knowing He has already secured your victory?

Reflection Questions for the Day:

1. How has God delivered you in the past?

2. Are you trusting Him for victory in your current struggles?

3. How can you share God's **teshuah** with others who need deliverance?

Day 324: Netzach (נֶ_צַ_ח)

- **Meaning:** Eternal Victory, Endurance, Everlasting Strength

- **Bible Reference:** 1 Samuel 15:29 – *"He who is the Glory of Israel does not lie or change His mind; for He is not a human being, that He should change His mind (netzach)."*

Message: Netzach signifies lasting victory, endurance, and the eternal nature of God's triumph. In battles, temporary victories may come and go, but God's **netzach** is unchanging and final. The cross seemed like defeat, but Jesus' resurrection was the ultimate **netzach**, proving that God's kingdom is unstoppable. Those who trust in the Lord will experience His **netzach**, standing firm even when trials come. God's promises do not fade, and His victory is never undone.

343

As believers, we are called to walk in **netzach**, living with eternal perspective and endurance. Are you holding onto the unshakable truth of God's eternal **netzach**?

Reflection Questions for the Day:

1. What does it mean to live in God's eternal victory?

2. Are you enduring in faith, even when trials come?

3. How can you encourage others with the assurance of God's **netzach**?

Day 325: Qum (קוּם)

- **Meaning:** Arise, Stand, Be Restored

- **Bible Reference:** Isaiah 60:1 – *"Arise (qum), shine, for your light has come, and the glory of the Lord rises upon you."*

Message: Qum is a call to action, urging God's people to rise up in faith, strength, and purpose. Throughout the Bible, God tells His servants to **qum**, calling them from despair into victory. Jesus often used the word **qum** when healing the sick, commanding them to rise and walk. The enemy tries to keep believers down through fear, doubt, and discouragement, but God calls us to **qum** in His power. When we arise in faith, we step into the destiny God has prepared for us. Victory is not just about winning battles but about standing firm and moving forward in God's plan. Are you responding to God's call to **qum**, rising in faith and strength?

Reflection Questions for the Day:

1. What areas of your life is God calling you to **qum**?

2. Are you letting fear or doubt keep you from standing in victory?

3. How can you encourage others to rise up in faith?

Day 326: Melek (מֶלֶךְ)

- **Meaning:** King, Ruler, Sovereign

- **Bible Reference:** Psalm 24:10 – *"Who is He, this King (melek) of glory? The Lord Almighty—He is the King of glory."*

Message: Melek refers to God as the sovereign King who reigns over all. While human kings rise and fall, God's kingdom is eternal, and His rule is just. Jesus came as the Servant **Melek**, showing that true leadership is marked by humility and love. Many expected a political ruler, but Jesus' kingship was about spiritual dominion, bringing salvation to the world. When we acknowledge Jesus as **Melek**, we submit to His authority and trust in His reign. Living under His kingship means aligning our lives with His will and seeking His kingdom first. Are you fully surrendered to Jesus as your **Melek**, following His rule in every area of your life?

Reflection Questions for the Day:

1. What does it mean to serve Jesus as King in your life?

2. Are you fully submitting to God's rule, or are you holding onto control?

3. How can you live as a faithful servant in God's kingdom?

Week 48 Conclusion

345

This week's words highlight the greatness of God's power and our victory in Him. **Gibbor** and **oz** remind us that He is mighty and strong. **Teshuah** and **netzach** assure us of His deliverance and eternal triumph. **Qum** calls us to rise up in faith, while **melek** declares His kingship. Trusting in God's victory means walking in confidence, knowing that nothing can defeat us when we stand in His strength. May we live each day with courage, faith, and a heart set on the ultimate triumph of our King.

Week 49: The Power of God's Wisdom and Understanding

Day 327: Chokhmah (חָכְמָה)

- **Meaning:** Wisdom, Skill, Insight

- **Bible Reference:** Proverbs 9:10 – *"The fear of the Lord is the beginning of wisdom (chokhmah), and knowledge of the Holy One is understanding."*

Message: Chokhmah is divine wisdom that goes beyond human intellect. The Bible teaches that true wisdom begins with the fear of the Lord, meaning reverence and obedience to Him. Solomon, known for his **chokhmah**, understood that wisdom is a gift from God, not something achieved through human effort alone. Jesus displayed perfect **chokhmah**, teaching profound truths that confounded religious leaders. God offers wisdom freely to those who seek Him with a humble heart. Applying **chokhmah** means making choices that honor God and lead to spiritual growth. Are you seeking God's **chokhmah**, or are you relying on your own understanding?

Reflection Questions for the Day:

1. What is the difference between worldly wisdom and divine **chokhmah**?

2. How can you seek God's wisdom in your daily decisions?

3. Are you open to learning and growing in God's **chokhmah**?

Day 328: Binah (בִּינָה)

- **Meaning:** Understanding, Discernment, Insight

- **Bible Reference:** Proverbs 2:3 – *"Indeed, if you call out for insight (binah) and cry aloud for understanding..."*

Message: Binah refers to discernment and the ability to grasp deeper truths. Many people have knowledge but lack **binah**, which allows them to apply what they know in meaningful ways. The Bible warns that without **binah**, people are easily deceived and led astray. Jesus displayed perfect **binah**, understanding people's hearts and responding with wisdom. Seeking **binah** requires humility, prayer, and dependence on God's Word. Those who cultivate **binah** grow in wisdom, making choices that align with God's will. Are you seeking to develop **binah**, allowing God to shape your understanding?

Reflection Questions for the Day:

1. How do you differentiate between knowledge and **binah**?

2. Are you asking God for discernment in your decisions?

3. How can you develop a deeper understanding of God's ways?

Day 329: Da'at (דַּעַת)

- **Meaning:** Knowledge, Awareness, Perception

- **Bible Reference:** Hosea 4:6 – *"My people are destroyed from lack of knowledge (da'at)."*

Message: Da'at is knowledge rooted in experience and relationship with God. The Bible warns that a lack of **da'at** leads to destruction, emphasizing the importance of knowing

God personally. Many people seek knowledge for personal gain, but true **da'at** comes from fearing the Lord and studying His Word. Jesus, the source of all **da'at**, invites us to grow in knowledge of Him through discipleship. God desires His people to have **da'at**, not just of Scripture, but of His nature, His love, and His will. Without **da'at**, people fall into spiritual confusion and false teachings. Are you pursuing **da'at**, seeking to know God more intimately?

Reflection Questions for the Day:

1. How does knowing God personally change your perspective?

2. Are you growing in **da'at**, or are you settling for shallow understanding?

3. What steps can you take to increase your knowledge of God?

Day 330: Sekhel (שֵׂ.כֶ.ל)

- **Meaning:** Prudence, Practical Wisdom, Common Sense

- **Bible Reference:** 1 Samuel 25:3 – *"Abigail was an intelligent (sekhel) and beautiful woman, but her husband was surly and mean in his dealings."*

Message: Sekhel refers to wisdom applied in practical ways—good judgment and common sense. Abigail demonstrated **sekhel** when she wisely intervened to prevent David from making a rash decision. Many people have knowledge but lack **sekhel**, leading to foolish choices despite knowing the truth. Jesus showed perfect **sekhel**, knowing when to speak, when to be silent, and how to answer difficult questions. Developing **sekhel** requires humility, patience, and a willingness to seek counsel. Godly **sekhel** helps us navigate life's challenges with wisdom and integrity. Are you practicing **sekhel**, making decisions that reflect God's wisdom?

Reflection Questions for the Day:

1. How can you develop greater wisdom in practical decisions?

2. Are you quick to act impulsively, or do you seek God's **sekhel** first?

3. How can you balance spiritual wisdom with practical application?

Day 331: Ormah (עָרְמָה)

- **Meaning:** Shrewdness, Craftiness, Strategic Wisdom

- **Bible Reference:** Proverbs 8:12 – *"I, wisdom, dwell together with prudence (ormah); I possess knowledge and discretion."*

Message: Ormah refers to strategic wisdom—the ability to think ahead and act wisely. The Bible praises **ormah** when used for good but warns against using it for deception. Jesus told His disciples to be "wise as serpents and innocent as doves," showing that wisdom and integrity go together. The enemy uses **ormah** for evil, but God calls His people to be shrewd in righteousness. Developing **ormah** requires discernment, prayer, and reliance on the Holy Spirit. A wise person considers the consequences of their actions and chooses the path of righteousness. Are you seeking godly **ormah**, using wisdom to navigate challenges?

Reflection Questions for the Day:

1. How can strategic wisdom help you avoid pitfalls?

2. Are you using **ormah** to make godly choices in challenging situations?

3. How can you balance wisdom with innocence in a world full of deception?

Day 332: Tushiyyah (תּוּשִׁ יָּ ה)

- **Meaning:** Sound Wisdom, Lasting Success, Solid Counsel

- **Bible Reference:** Job 12:13 – *"To God belong wisdom (tushiyyah) and power; counsel and understanding are His."*

Message: Tushiyyah refers to wisdom that leads to success and stability. Unlike temporary cleverness, **tushiyyah** is wisdom that produces lasting, godly results. Throughout Scripture, those who sought God's **tushiyyah** prospered, while those who ignored it faced destruction. Solomon ruled with **tushiyyah**, making decisions that brought peace and prosperity to Israel. Jesus demonstrated **tushiyyah** in His teachings, providing life-changing counsel. Seeking **tushiyyah** means asking for wisdom that works in real life, not just theoretical knowledge. Are you pursuing wisdom that leads to lasting success, or are you making choices based on temporary desires?

Reflection Questions for the Day:

1. How can wisdom lead to lasting success in your life?

2. Are you applying God's **tushiyyah**, or just hearing it?

3. What steps can you take to grow in sound wisdom?

Week 49 Conclusion

This week's words emphasize the importance of seeking God's wisdom and understanding in all aspects of life. **Chokhmah** and **binah** highlight the depth of divine wisdom, while **da'at** calls us to know God personally. **Sekhel** and **ormah** focus on practical and strategic wisdom, guiding our daily decisions. **Tushiyyah** reminds us that true wisdom brings lasting success, not just temporary gain. Walking in God's wisdom leads to peace, discernment, and victory in life's challenges. May we seek His wisdom daily, trusting in His guidance and applying His truth to every area of our lives.

Week 50: The Power of God's Love and Compassion

Day 333: Ahavah (אַהֲבָה)

- **Meaning:** Love, Deep Affection, Devotion

- **Bible Reference:** Deuteronomy 6:5 – *"Love (ahavah) the Lord your God with all your heart and with all your soul and with all your strength."*

Message: Ahavah is more than just a feeling; it is a deep, committed love that involves action. The Bible teaches that God's **ahavah** is steadfast and unchanging, not dependent on human performance. In Deuteronomy, God commands His people to love Him with all their heart, soul, and strength, showing that **ahavah** is a choice and a commitment. Jesus demonstrated the greatest **ahavah** by laying down His life for us. Love is the foundation of all relationships—with God and with others. True **ahavah** is sacrificial, patient, and kind, mirroring God's love. Are you practicing true **ahavah**, loving God and others with sincerity and action?

Reflection Questions for the Day:

1. How does God's **ahavah** impact your daily life?

2. Are you showing sacrificial love to those around you?

3. How can you deepen your love for God and others?

Day 334: Chesed (חֶסֶד)

- **Meaning:** Lovingkindness, Mercy, Unfailing Love

- **Bible Reference:** Lamentations 3:22 – *"Because of the Lord's great love (chesed) we are not consumed, for His compassions never fail."*

Message: Chesed is one of the most beautiful words in the Bible, describing God's covenant love and mercy. It is a steadfast, loyal love that remains faithful despite human failure. Throughout Scripture, God's **chesed** is evident in His patience and forgiveness toward Israel. Jesus embodied **chesed**, showing mercy to sinners, healing the broken, and sacrificing Himself for humanity. This kind of love is not based on emotions but on a covenant commitment. We are called to show **chesed** to others, extending grace, forgiveness, and kindness. Are you reflecting God's **chesed** in your relationships, loving with patience and faithfulness?

Reflection Questions for the Day:

1. How have you experienced God's **chesed** in your life?

2. Are you extending **chesed** to others, even when they don't deserve it?

3. What practical ways can you demonstrate lovingkindness today?

Day 335: Racham (ר_ח_ם)

- **Meaning:** Compassion, Tender Mercy, Deep Care

- **Bible Reference:** Isaiah 49:15 – *"Can a mother forget the baby at her breast and have no compassion (racham) on the child she has borne? Though she may forget, I will not forget you!"*

Message: Racham is derived from the Hebrew word for "womb," signifying a deep, nurturing love and compassion. God's **racham** is compared to a mother's love for her child, showing the intensity of His care for us. Even when the world rejects or forgets us, God's **racham** remains constant. Jesus displayed **racham** when He wept for Jerusalem and had compassion on the suffering. True **racham** moves beyond emotions—it leads to action in helping those in need. As

356

recipients of God's **racham**, we are called to be compassionate toward others. Are you cultivating a heart of **racham**, reflecting God's mercy and care?

Reflection Questions for the Day:

1. How has God's **racham** comforted you in difficult times?

2. Are you showing compassion to others as God has shown it to you?

3. What actions can you take to express deeper compassion in your life?

Day 336: Dod (דּוֹד)

- **Meaning:** Beloved, Affectionate Love

- **Bible Reference:** Song of Solomon 5:16 – *"His mouth is sweetness itself; he is altogether lovely. This is my beloved (dod), this is my friend, daughters of Jerusalem."*

Message: Dod is a term of deep affection, often used to describe the intimate love between a husband and wife. The Song of Solomon expresses this kind of love, symbolizing the relationship between Christ and His Church. God desires an intimate relationship with His people, one that is marked by closeness, passion, and devotion. Jesus, as the Bridegroom, calls us to love Him with the same intensity. **Dod** teaches us that love is not just duty—it is delight and joy in relationship. Loving God should not feel like an obligation but a privilege. Are you growing in intimacy with God, seeing Him as your **dod**, your Beloved?

Reflection Questions for the Day:

1. How can you deepen your relationship with God in intimacy and devotion?

2. Do you see your walk with Christ as a duty or as a joy-filled relationship?

3. What steps can you take to strengthen your love for God?

Day 337: Tov Lev (טוֹב לֵב)

- **Meaning:** A Good Heart, Generosity, Kindness

- **Bible Reference:** Proverbs 11:25 – *"A generous person will prosper; whoever refreshes others will be refreshed."*

Message: Tov lev describes a person with a good heart, one who is generous and kind. In Scripture, generosity is a sign of a heart that reflects God's love. Jesus praised those who gave selflessly, showing that true love is expressed through giving. A **tov lev** does not hold back but looks for ways to bless others. Generosity is not just about money—it is about time, kindness, and care. When we live with a **tov lev**, we reflect God's nature and experience the joy of giving. Are you cultivating a **tov lev**, allowing God's love to flow through you in generosity?

Reflection Questions for the Day:

1. How does generosity reflect God's love?

2. Are you practicing generosity in your daily life?

3. What is one way you can show kindness today?

Day 338: Yedid (יְדִיד)

- **Meaning:** Dear Friend, Cherished One, Close Companion

- **Bible Reference:** Psalm 127:2 – *"He gives sleep to His beloved (yedid)."*

Message: Yedid is a term of deep friendship and cherished love. The Bible speaks of God calling His people **yedid**, His beloved friends and companions. Jesus told His disciples, *"I no longer call you servants, but friends,"* showing His personal love for them. Being God's **yedid** means living in closeness with Him, knowing we are deeply loved. Friendship with God is a privilege that should not be taken lightly. As His **yedid**, we are invited into deep fellowship, where we find peace and rest. Are you embracing your identity as God's **yedid**, knowing you are cherished and loved?

Reflection Questions for the Day:

1. How does knowing you are God's **yedid** change your perspective?

2. Are you investing in a deeper friendship with God?

3. How can you show love and friendship to others?

Week 50 Conclusion

This week's words reveal the depth and richness of God's love. **Ahavah** and **chesed** remind us of His unbreakable love and kindness, while **racham** shows His deep, compassionate care. **Dod** speaks of the intimate love God desires with His people, and **yedid** reminds us that we are His cherished friends. **Tov lev** challenges us to live generously, and **dod** calls us to delight in our relationship with Him. Love is not just something we receive—it is something we give, reflecting God's character to the world.

Week 51: The Power of God's Peace and Rest

Day 339: Shalom (שָׁלוֹם)

- **Meaning:** Peace, Wholeness, Harmony, Complete Well-being

- **Bible Reference:** Isaiah 26:3 – *"You will keep in perfect peace (shalom) those whose minds are steadfast, because they trust in You."*

Message: Shalom is more than the absence of conflict—it represents complete well-being, wholeness, and harmony with God. The biblical concept of **shalom** encompasses inner peace, restored relationships, and security in God's presence. Jesus, the Prince of **Shalom**, came to reconcile humanity to God, bringing deep peace through His sacrifice. True **shalom** comes from trusting in God's sovereignty, even in difficult circumstances. The world offers temporary peace, but God's **shalom** is eternal and unshakable. When we walk in **shalom**, we reflect His presence to those around us. Are you living in God's **shalom**, allowing Him to guard your heart and mind?

Reflection Questions for the Day:

1. How can you cultivate **shalom** in your heart and home?

2. Are you trusting in God's peace, or are you consumed by worry?

3. How can you share God's **shalom** with those who are struggling?

Day 340: Nuach (נוּחַ)

- **Meaning:** Rest, Settle, Abide

- **Bible Reference:** Exodus 33:14 – *"My Presence will go with you, and I will give you rest (nuach)."*

Message: Nuach describes a deep, abiding rest that comes from being in God's presence. After creating the world, God **nuach** on the seventh day, setting an example of holy rest. True rest is not just physical relaxation but spiritual renewal found in Him. Jesus invites us to come to Him for **nuach**, to find peace in surrender and trust. The world glorifies busyness, but God calls us to slow down and abide in Him. When we rest in God's promises, we are strengthened for life's challenges. Are you prioritizing **nuach**, finding true rest in God's presence?

Reflection Questions for the Day:

1. How can you create intentional space for **nuach** in your life?

2. Are you resting in God's promises, or are you striving in your own strength?

3. How does resting in God prepare you for challenges ahead?

Day 341: Menuchah (מְ נוּחָ ה)

- **Meaning:** Stillness, Restful Dwelling, Tranquility

- **Bible Reference:** Psalm 23:2 – *"He makes me lie down in green pastures, He leads me beside quiet (menuchah) waters."*

Message: Menuchah is the quiet, still rest that brings refreshment to the soul. David experienced **menuchah** when he found peace in God's provision and protection. God's Sabbath was established as a time of **menuchah**, inviting His people to cease from striving and enjoy His presence. Jesus demonstrated **menuchah**, withdrawing often to pray and be with the Father. In a world of noise and busyness, we need to seek **menuchah**—to be still and know that He is God. When we embrace **menuchah**, we grow in faith, knowing that God's care is sufficient. Are you allowing time for **menuchah**, resting in the stillness of God's presence?

Reflection Questions for the Day:

1. When was the last time you truly rested in God's presence?

2. How can you practice **menuchah** in your daily life?

3. Are you allowing distractions to steal your peace and rest?

Day 342: Sha'an (שָׁאַן)

- **Meaning:** To Be Secure, At Ease, Unafraid

- **Bible Reference:** Proverbs 1:33 – *"Whoever listens to Me will live in safety and be at ease (sha'an), without fear of harm."*

Message: Sha'an describes a deep security that comes from trusting in God's protection. Fear and anxiety dominate the world, but those who walk with God can live with confidence. The Bible repeatedly reminds us to "fear not," because God is our refuge and strength. Jesus reassured His disciples not to be troubled, for He had overcome the world. When we develop a **sha'an** mindset, we rely on God's promises rather than fear's whispers. Trusting in God's control brings peace beyond understanding. Are you resting in **sha'an**, allowing God to replace your fears with His security?

Reflection Questions for the Day:

1. What fears do you need to surrender to God?

2. How can faith in God's promises help you live with **sha'an**?

3. Are you walking in confidence, knowing God is your protector?

Day 343: Shavat (שָׁ_בַ_ת)

- **Meaning:** To Cease, Stop, Rest from Work
- **Bible Reference:** Genesis 2:2 – *"By the seventh day God had finished the work He had been doing; so on the seventh day He rested (shavat) from all His work."*

Message: Shavat means to stop and rest, recognizing that we are not defined by our work but by God's grace. God Himself **shavat** after creation, setting an example for us to rest and reflect. The Sabbath was given as a gift, not as a burden, inviting us to pause and worship. Jesus emphasized that true Sabbath rest is found in Him, freeing us from striving. In a culture that rewards endless work, we must embrace the discipline of **shavat**. Rest is not laziness—it is an act of faith, trusting that God is in control. Are you practicing **shavat**, intentionally stopping to worship and be refreshed?

Reflection Questions for the Day:

1. Do you make time to **shavat**, or are you always busy?

2. How can practicing Sabbath rest deepen your relationship with God?

3. Are you trusting that God is at work even when you rest?

Day 344: Rega (רֶ_גַ_ע)

- **Meaning:** A Moment, A Brief Pause, Rest from Turmoil

- **Bible Reference:** Isaiah 54:7 – *"For a brief moment (rega) I abandoned you, but with deep compassion I will bring you back."*

Message: Rega reminds us that even in the midst of trouble, God provides moments of peace and restoration. Life is filled with storms, but God offers **rega**, brief pauses where we experience His comfort. Sometimes, all it takes is a moment in His presence to renew our strength. Jesus took moments of solitude to reconnect with the Father, demonstrating the power of sacred pauses. God's mercy is revealed in **rega**, as He never leaves His people in suffering forever. Even in trials, there is a **rega** of grace—a glimpse of God's peace. Are you taking time to embrace the **rega** moments of rest and renewal that God provides?

Reflection Questions for the Day:

1. How can you find moments of peace in your daily routine?

2. Are you recognizing the **rega** moments God gives to restore you?

3. What distractions keep you from experiencing God's **rega**?

Week 51 Conclusion

This week's words reveal God's deep desire for His people to live in peace and rest. **Shalom** represents complete well-being, while **nuach** and **menuchah** emphasize dwelling in God's presence. **Sha'an** calls us to security in Him, and **shavat** teaches the importance of resting from work. **Rega** reminds us that even brief moments in God's presence bring renewal. True rest is found not in inactivity, but in abiding with God and trusting in His provision. May we embrace His peace, making space for rest, renewal, and deeper intimacy with Him.

Week 52: The Power of God's Eternal Kingdom

Day 345: Malkut (מַ_לְ_כוּת)

- **Meaning:** Kingdom, Reign, Sovereignty

- **Bible Reference:** Psalm 145:13 – *"Your kingdom (malkut) is an everlasting kingdom, and Your dominion endures through all generations."*

Message: Malkut refers to the rule and reign of God, which is eternal and unshakable. Unlike earthly kingdoms that rise and fall, God's **malkut** will last forever. Jesus preached about the **malkut** of God, calling people to repent and enter into His divine rule. Those who seek His **malkut** first will experience His provision, peace, and purpose. As citizens of God's **malkut**, we are called to live differently, prioritizing His will over worldly pursuits. His kingdom is not about power or status but about righteousness, peace, and joy in the Holy Spirit. Are you actively seeking God's **malkut**, living as a faithful servant in His kingdom?

Reflection Questions for the Day:

1. What does it mean to be part of God's **malkut**?

2. Are you prioritizing His kingdom over worldly desires?

3. How can you actively live as a representative of God's **malkut**?

Day 346: Adon (אָדוֹן)

- **Meaning:** Lord, Master, Ruler

- **Bible Reference:** Malachi 1:6 – *"If I am a master (adon), where is the respect due Me?"*

Message: Adon means "lord" or "master," signifying God's supreme authority. Throughout Scripture, God is referred to as **Adonai**, the sovereign ruler over all creation. Jesus is our **Adon**, calling us to surrender our lives under His lordship. Many acknowledge Jesus as Savior but struggle to submit to Him as **Adon**. True discipleship means recognizing Him as our Master in all areas of life. Surrendering to God's **adon** leads to freedom, for His rule is just and His ways are perfect. Are you fully surrendering to God as your **Adon**, allowing Him to lead your life?

Reflection Questions for the Day:

1. What does it mean for Jesus to be your **Adon**?

2. Are there areas in your life that you struggle to surrender to His lordship?

3. How can you live in full submission to God's authority?

Day 347: Yeshua (יְשׁוּעַ)

- **Meaning:** Salvation, Deliverance, Rescue

- **Bible Reference:** Matthew 1:21 – *"She will give birth to a son, and you are to give Him the name Jesus (Yeshua), because He will save His people from their sins."*

Message: Yeshua, the Hebrew name of Jesus, means "salvation" and reflects His mission to save humanity. The name **Yeshua** embodies God's plan of redemption, bringing freedom from sin and eternal life. Jesus is not just a historical figure; He is the living **Yeshua**, who still saves and delivers today. His salvation is complete—spiritually, emotionally, and even physically. Many look for salvation in temporary

370

things, but only **Yeshua** provides eternal security. Trusting in **Yeshua** means placing our full confidence in Him, not in our own efforts. Are you fully embracing the salvation that **Yeshua** offers, allowing Him to transform your life?

Reflection Questions for the Day:

1. What does **Yeshua** mean to you personally?

2. Have you fully accepted the salvation Jesus offers?

3. How can you share the message of **Yeshua** with others?

Day 348: Mishpat (מִ שְׁ פָּ ט)

- **Meaning:** Justice, Righteous Judgment, Law

- **Bible Reference:** Isaiah 30:18 – *"For the Lord is a God of justice (mishpat). Blessed are all who wait for Him!"*

Message: Mishpat is the foundation of God's righteousness, representing His perfect justice. While human justice is often flawed, God's **mishpat** is always fair, merciful, and true. Throughout Scripture, God commands His people to practice **mishpat**, caring for the oppressed and upholding righteousness. Jesus, the Righteous Judge, will one day establish perfect **mishpat**, restoring all things. Living under God's **mishpat** means aligning our actions with His truth and treating others with fairness. When we trust in His justice, we can let go of revenge and trust that He will make all things right. Are you living according to God's **mishpat**, reflecting His justice in your actions?

Reflection Questions for the Day:

1. How does God's **mishpat** bring hope to a broken world?

2. Are you practicing justice and fairness in your relationships?

3. How can you trust God's **mishpat**, even when life seems unfair?

Day 349: Simchah (שִׂמְחָה)

- **Meaning:** Joy, Gladness, Celebration

- **Bible Reference:** Nehemiah 8:10 – *"Do not grieve, for the joy (simchah) of the Lord is your strength."*

Message: Simchah is the deep joy that comes from knowing and walking with God. Unlike fleeting happiness, **simchah** is rooted in faith and trust in God's goodness. The Bible commands believers to rejoice always, for **simchah** is a choice, not just an emotion. Jesus brings **simchah** to those who follow Him, turning mourning into dancing. The enemy seeks to steal our **simchah**, but God calls us to live in His joy, despite circumstances. Worship, gratitude, and obedience cultivate **simchah**, keeping our hearts strong and focused on Him. Are you walking in the **simchah** of the Lord, letting His joy be your strength?

Reflection Questions for the Day:

1. What is the difference between happiness and **simchah**?

2. How can you choose joy even in difficult times?

3. Are you reflecting God's joy to those around you?

Day 350: Kavod (כָּבוֹד)

- **Meaning:** Glory, Honor, Weightiness of God's Presence

- **Bible Reference:** Habakkuk 2:14 – *"For the earth will be filled with the knowledge of the glory (kavod) of the Lord as the waters cover the sea."*

Message: Kavod represents the overwhelming glory of God's presence. When God's **kavod** filled the temple, it was so powerful that the priests could not stand. Jesus displayed God's **kavod**, revealing His divine nature through miracles, teachings, and His resurrection. As believers, we are called to reflect God's **kavod**, living in a way that brings Him honor. One day, the whole earth will be filled with His **kavod**, and every knee will bow before Him. Walking in God's **kavod** means living with reverence, knowing we carry His presence. Are you seeking to live for God's **kavod**, honoring Him in all you do?

Reflection Questions for the Day:

1. How does God's **kavod** impact your worship and daily life?

2. Are you reflecting His glory in your words and actions?

3. How can you live in a way that brings honor to God?

Week 52 Conclusion

This week's words remind us of the eternal nature of God's reign. **Malkut** assures us that His kingdom will never end, while **Adon** calls us to surrender to His lordship. **Yeshua** is the foundation of our salvation, and **mishpat** reveals God's perfect justice. **Simchah** brings joy in our journey, while **kavod** reminds us to live for His glory. God's kingdom is not of this world, yet we are called to live as its citizens, honoring Him in all we do. As we finish this year of learning, may we continue to seek His kingdom, live in His truth, and shine His light to the world.

Final Reflection: A Year of Growing in God's Word

Over the past 52 weeks, we have explored 365 Hebrew words that reveal the richness of God's character, promises, and purpose. Each word has given us a deeper understanding of His love, faithfulness, power, wisdom, and presence.

We began by learning about **God's nature**, discovering words like **El Shaddai (God Almighty)**, **Adonai (Lord and Master)**, and **Kavod (Glory)**—reminders that God is supreme, holy, and worthy of worship. As we moved through the weeks, we saw His **compassion** in words like **Racham (Mercy)** and **Chesed (Lovingkindness)**, showing His relentless grace toward us.

We studied the importance of **obedience and wisdom**, with words such as **Chokhmah (Wisdom)**, **Binah (Understanding)**, and **Dabar (Word, Promise)**—teaching us to seek God's guidance in all things. We also learned about **God's faithfulness and restoration**, through words like **Teshuvah (Repentance)**, **Shuv (Return to God)**, and **Tikkun (Restoration)**—reminding us that God is always ready to forgive and renew.

As we explored **God's protection and strength**, words like **Magen (Shield)**, **Gibbor (Mighty Warrior)**, and **Rapha (Healer)** assured us that He fights for us and heals our brokenness. We also discovered the importance of **rest and peace** through words like **Shalom (Complete Peace)**, **Nuach (Rest in God)**, and **Sha'an (Security and Confidence)**—reminding us that our true peace is found in Him.

Finally, we closed with words that point us to **God's eternal kingdom—Malkut (Kingdom of God), Yeshua (Salvation)**, and **Simchah (Joy in the Lord)**. These words call us to live as faithful citizens of His kingdom, reflecting His glory and sharing His truth with the world.

As this journey comes to an end, let this be the beginning of a lifetime of seeking God through His Word. May we continue to meditate on these truths, apply them to our daily lives, and grow in faith.

Questions for Reflection:

1. Which words from this study impacted you the most, and why?

2. How has your understanding of God deepened through learning these Hebrew words?

3. In what ways can you continue to seek God's wisdom and truth beyond this study?

4. How can you use what you've learned to encourage and teach others about God's Word?

5. What commitments will you make to grow spiritually in the coming year?

May God bless you abundantly as you continue to walk in His truth and seek His presence every day. **Shalom and blessings!**

Appendix - Words Multiple times

Words are arranged based on the theme discussed every week. Below words are repeated multiple time, as the meaning of these words relevant to the theme of that week.

Word	Repeated	Word	Repeated
Shalom	7	Lechem	2
Chesed	5	Shakan	2
Emunah	5	Gibbor	2
Binah	5	Shuv	2
Rachamim	4	Chadesh	2
Panim	4	Selah	2
Yeshuah	4	Yare	2
Shekinah	4	Sha'an	2
Dabar	4	Kaphar	2
Chanan	4	Selichah	2
Or	4	Simchah	2
Sekhel	4	Seter	2
Da'at	4	Chazaq	2
Tzur	3	Yireh	2

Derekh	3	Emun	2
Mishpat	3	Tamim	2
Zakar	3	Lev Chadash	2
Ruach	3	Brit	2
Menuchah	3	Tzedakah	2
Ne'eman	3	Yeshua	2
Go'el	3	Lev	2
Nachalah	3	Yirah	2
Ormah	3	Berit	2
Tushiyyah	3	Avodah	2
Tahor	3	Zamar	2
Netzach	3	Yadah	2
Emet	3	Yeshivah	2
Magen	3	Anan	2
Tikvah	3	Shefa	2
Qavah	3	Chokhmah	2
Makom	3	Oz	2

Kavod	3	Ma'oz	2
Ahavah	3	Yashar	2
Machseh	3	Qara	2
Qadosh	3	Shavat	2
Tehillah	3	Dod	2

www.ingramcontent.com/pod-product-compliance
Lightning Source LLC
LaVergne TN
LVHW051540080426
835510LV00020B/2791